Survivors
OF THE SEA

Sole Survivors OF THE SEA

by James E. Wise Jr.

BLUEJACKET BOOKS

Naval Institute Press
Annapolis, Maryland

Naval Institute Press
291 Wood Road
Annapolis, MD 21402

Originally published by the Nautical and Aviation Publishing Company of America, Inc.

First Naval Institute Press paperback edition published in 2008.

Library of Congress Cataloging-in-Publication Data
Wise, James E., 1930–
Sole survivors of the sea / James E. Wise, Jr.
p. cm.
Originally published: Baltimore, Md. : Nautical & Aviation Pub., c1994.
Includes bibliographical references.
ISBN 978-1-59114-943-9 (alk. paper)
1. World War, 1939-1945—Naval operations. 2 . Shipwrecks. 3. Survival after airplane accidents, shipwrecks, etc. I. Title.
D770.W55 2007
940.54′5—dc22

2007034727

Printed in the United States of America on acid-free paper ∞

14 13 12 11 10 09 08 9 8 7 6 5 4 3 2

For my daughters: Allison, Julie, and Jacqueline

CONTENTS

FOREWORD

While researching materials for another book (*Shooting the War, of a World War II U-Boat Officer*, Naval Institute Press, Annapolis, 1994), I came across an incident in World War II that told of a sole survivor of a naval warship sunk during a fierce battle in the Pacific. The story was so intriguing that I wondered if there were, perhaps, other sole survivors of similar incidents. The thought lingered with me for several months.

Finally, I decided to dig further into the subject, and with the help of various historical archive sources, sole survivor incidents began to surface.

The first concerned a 17-year-old girl who alone survived a plane crash in the Peruvian jungle in December of 1972. Ninety-one of her fellow passengers perished, including her mother who was sitting beside her. The frail survivor managed to find her way to civilization after nine days in the wilderness. After regaining her health, she pondered deeply about her survival. ''Why me?'' she asked. ''And why not my mother?''

As I found more incidents of sole survivors I tried to gain a better perspective on why certain people survived catastrophes against all odds. Many were lucky. They were at the right place at the right time. Others seemed to possess such a tenacious will to live that they were able to endure unbelievable hardships and survive while others perished. Still others have never been able to find a satisfactory explanation for their good fortune.

I became so intrigued by the subject that I decided to chronicle a number of these stories. As a naval historian I stayed in familiar waters and selected those who survived the perils of the sea. Most occurred during World War II when the navies and merchant fleets of many nations, friend and enemy, roamed the seas of the world. To my surprise many involved submarines, especially German U-Boats.

Unfortunately, I was not able to interview many of the survivors since most have since sailed on to waters beyond the horizon. However, all accounts are true in their content. Official government documents, a wide array of historical reference sources, and, where possible, correspondence with survivor family members have been used.

Not being able to ask the question, "Why me?" of the survivors, I leave it up to the reader to answer this complex question while reading through the individual stories. After finishing the book, most readers will have found their own answers.

Captain James E. Wise, Jr., USN (Ret.)
Alexandria, Virginia

ACKNOWLEDGEMENTS

I am indebted to a number of people who helped in making this book possible. I'd particularly like to thank Jack Taylor, ex-Royal Navy man, who survived U-boat sinkings while serving aboard British merchant ships during World War II. Also, I am indebted to Lieutenant Commander A. Hague VRD*RNR (Ret.) for his invaluable assistance throughout this project.

Others in the U.K. who deserve my gratitude include: Lionel Wheble, Maritime Royal Artillery Old Comrades Association; Terence C. Charman and Allison E. Duffield, Imperial War Museum; R.S. Horne, Marine Accident Investigations Branch; H.L. Cooper, Trinity House Lighthouse Service; Major J.D. Braisby RA (Ret.), Editor of *Gunner* magazine; Warrant Officer Writer B.J. Wead, Royal Navy, *HMS Nelson*; Brigadier K.A. Timbers, Royal Artillery Historical Trust; David Ashby, Naval Historical Branch, Ministry of Defence; Mrs. C. Freeman, General Register and Record Office of Shipping and Seamen, Department of Transportation; and P. Jarman, Guildhall Library.

I am most grateful to Mrs. Richard Ayers who shared information about her late husband with me. Also, Mr. Emrys Jones, relative of Captain Robert Jones, who provided most of the material used in the chapter, *The Henry Stanley*.

Prof. Dr. Jurgen Rohwer, Bibliothek fur Zeitgeschichte, as in the past, graciously took time out of his busy schedule to assist us. Horst Bredow, Director of U-Boot Archive in Cuxhaven, Germany, provided vital data and several of the photographic illustrations. And, my good friend and co-author of another book,

Otto Giese, former U-boat Watch Officer, was ever present to lend a helping hand. My thanks also go to Herr Jamans, Bundesarchiv/Miltararchiv, Freiburg, Germany.

Regarding the lone survivors of the Italian submarine *Archimede* and the car ferry *Moby Prince,* I am indebted to Amm. Div. Renato Sicurezza, Ufficio Storico della Marina Militare, for his timely assistance.

Here in the U.S. there are many, many to thank for their professional expertise and research assistance. For the Poon Lim story I am indebted to Ruthanne Lum McCunn for her information and book on Lim's experience, *Sole Survivor.* Also, Johnny Yee of the Chinese American Historical Society was most helpful in providing me with a vast array of materials on this unique story. Naval historian Eddie Rumpf proved to be an encyclopedia of information about sole survivors during World War II.

I am grateful to The Great Lakes Historical Society for the valuable data they provided on Captain Walter Grashaw and his harrowing experience on Lake Erie in 1916. I am also indebted to his son, Nelson, who gave me further personal insights on his father, an extraordinary sea Captain.

I'd also like to extend my thanks to Timothy Mulligan and Rebecca Livingstone, National Archives, for their tireless pursuit of information on my behalf. And to my German translator, Marianne K. Driscoll, who worked with me throughout this project, a special "Vielen Danka". Also, I'd like to extend a special appreciation to Mrs. Susan Bacs, whose administrative skill in transposing our scribblings into a finished manuscript has been invaluable in this venture.

Finally, staff personnel at the Operational Archives of the Naval Historical Center, Washington, D.C., deserve special mention for their assistance in this effort. I'd like to cite their names since each one played a key role in researching information for this book. They are Kathleen Lloyd, John Hodges, and Gina Akers. Also, many thanks to V. Daniel Hunt for his expert advice and personal encouragement during the writing of this book.

CHAPTER ONE

STICK IT, MISTER!*

The voices of children reached him from high above. They were calling to him with high pitched voices, ''Stick it, mister! Stick it mister!'' In a last, desperate effort he had wrapped a sudden found rope around himself and felt his body being pulled through a crashing surf. He was unconscious when his exhausted body reached the shore at Lizard Point some 60 miles south of Plymouth, England. Second Officer Richard H. Ayres had survived after thirteen days at sea fighting frigid gales and rolling seas in a lifeboat that once held 32 survivors of the British merchant ship *Gairsoppa*. *U-101* under the command of Kapitänleutnant Ernst Mengersen, holder of the Knight's Cross, sent the *Gairsoppa* to the bottom 300 miles southwest of Galway, Ireland February 17, 1941. Second Officer Ayres was the only survivor of the ill fated ship.[1]

*English slang for ''Hang in there!''

Second Officer Richard H. Ayers - (Mrs. Richard H. Ayers)

Owned by the British India Steam Navigation Company, the 5,000 ton *Gairsoppa* was one of many British merchantmen that risked death at sea to save Great Britain during the early days of World War II. Assaulted from the air day and night by the German *Luftwaffe,* the country looked to the sea and the merchant convoys for survival. In their fierce struggle to reach port cities, thousands of British seamen lost their lives to U-boat attacks. In February 1941 alone, thirty-eight British merchant ships totaling 203,212 tons were lost.[2]

The *Gairsoppa* started her final journey in December 1940 when she was cleared by the port authorities at Calcutta to proceed to the home islands via the Cape of Good Hope. Ladened with gunny bags, tea, and pig iron, the ship made refuelling stops at Colombo, Durban, and Cape Town. Her next port of call, Freetown, Sierra Leone, was a beehive of shipping activity. Here, convoys formed for their journey north to the United Kingdom. *Gairsoppa* was ordered to join a slow, eight knot convoy, SL.64.

SL.64 steamed out of Freetown in late January. The ships posted lookouts day and night and blacked out at night. Convoy escorts roamed in and around the convoy in search of underwater prowlers. As the ships reached the northern latitudes, the winds increased and the ocean swells deepened. *Gairsoppa,* with her heavy cargo of pig iron, had to carry more steam to keep up with the convoy. As the weather worsened, the *Gairsoppa*'s skipper, Captain Hyland, informed the convoy commodore that his bunkers were running low and that he wouldn't have enough fuel to stay with the convoy and reach their destination. The commodore gave Hyland permission to proceed independently and sail for Galway in Southern Ireland.

On February 14, the *Gairsoppa* departed the convoy in heavy seas. The next day the master was able to get a navigational fix using the sun. The ship was steady on course for Galway.

The following morning an unidentified four-engined aircraft was sighted circling the ship. After an hour or so it disappeared. As darkness fell that day, the winds rose to gale force and the air became frigid. The blacked-out ship lumbered through the turbulent sea, its lookouts scanning the darkness for any sign of the enemy. At about 2230 hours a sudden explosion occurred in the No. 2 hold. The impact of the detonation caused the foremast to break and crash to the deck. The mast held both wireless antennae, thus the ship was immediately cut off from the outside world.

The crew rushed to their abandon ship stations as the ship began to slow down and water began to rush over its bow. The fo'c'sle of the doomed vessel was quickly underwater. Captain Hyland, sensing the ship was going under fast, ordered his men to abandon ship. Fire and smoke from hold No. 2 added to the confusion as British and Indian seamen began to climb into lifeboats which had been previously slung out in preparation for such an emergency.

Second Officer Ayres reached his station only to be pinned down by machine gun fire coming from the U-boat somewhere out in the darkened night. He and his comrades flattened themselves out on the deck as bullets sprayed the area around them. To their good fortune the heavy fire cut the lifeboat hoist lines and the boat fell into the sea, right side up. The crew, which included lascars (East Indian sailors), jumped into the boat and pushed themselves away from the sinking vessel. By now the ship was down by its head with its stern clear out of the water. Despite their efforts, Ayres and his crew had drifted toward the stern and were nearly struck by the ship's still spinning propeller. Using their oars they were able to avoid disaster and move a hundred yards or so away from the sinking ship. Twenty minutes later the *Gairsoppa* disappeared. Ayres and his shipmates scanned the darkness for other boats. Nothing was sighted, no voices could be heard. They were alone. The rest of the ship's crew had been lost.

Ayres took count of his fellow survivors. There were thirty-two in all. Twenty-three were Indians. Since he was the only one experienced in handling a small boat, he took charge. Using a makeshift sea anchor, he kept the boat headed into the wind during the remaining night hours. The following morning the winds continued to sweep the churning sea. He scanned the horizon for other boats and found that they were alone and adrift since they had lost their rudder when the boat dropped into the sea from its davits.

Ayres immediately took stock of the supplies stocked in the boat. There were six tins of biscuits, twenty-four tins of condensed milk, and two casks of water, one of which had been damaged and was half full. He announced that each man would be allowed two dippers of water a day, one during the day, the other at night. Each ration measured about one-half of a pint.

The Indians were of immediate concern since they were not clothed to withstand the frigid cold of the Atlantic winter. Winds would often gust to fifty miles an hour, causing them to huddle closely together to share their body warmth. Ayres ordered them forward in the boat where he fixed a canvas shelter for them. He gave them all available blankets and other crewmen gave them additional clothing to ward off the cold.

The boat continually took on water in the rough seas. The men hastily bailed the water over the side, lest the boat become swamped. Once the Indians were sheltered, Ayres and the other men labored to build a similar cover over the aft end of the boat to protect them from the icy sea spray that swirled around the boat.

The biscuits were found to be hard as rocks and Ayres ordered the men to soften them with their water rations. Many of the crew tried to eat the lead-like biscuits, others just discarded them. Though many asked for more water to wash the biscuits down, Ayres remained steadfast in his rationing schedule.

After a day or so of drifting and no rescue vessels in sight, Ayres decided to set sail and run before a westerly gale. He set the mast for full sail and used an oar for steering the vessel. He estimated that England lay to the east some several hundred miles away.

By the fourth day the men were exhausted and the Indians appeared to be especially affected by the ordeal. They continually craved for more water and when denied additional rations resorted to drinking salt water. This had disastrous results. Within a short time, they began to die. In the first seven days, sixteen of them succumbed and their bodies were gently pushed over the side. Ayres was helpless to save them.

On the eighth day they ran out of water. The entire crew was subdued. The Indians no longer clamored for more water, they were too weak to move. Some suffered from severe frostbite and a few showed signs of gangrene infection. Although the situation looked bleak, Ayres was still optimistic that they would make it. He just wouldn't accept defeat. At the start of the ordeal he was a fit thirty-one-year-old man known for his leadership and self control. Taking care of his charges for 8 days with little sleep, he began to weaken and, like the others, suffered from frostbite.

Additional members of the crew began to die around the ninth day. Only the radio officer, a gunner named Norman Thomas, and Ayres were able to take their turns sailing the boat. On the tenth day a squall passed over them and they dropped their mainsail, hoping to catch precious droplets. The respite was short lived since little water was captured. Their lives again began to ebb away. Rain came again on the next day, but it was too brief and not enough was collected to satisfy their parched bodies.

Four Indians and three other crewmen remained alive by the twelfth day. Some were semi-conscious, all somehow clung to life. Ayres courageously sailed the craft through raging gales and thundering seas. His spirit unbroken, he was determined to save the lives of those remaining. He was convinced that land lay just ahead.

Then, in the early morning light of the thirteenth day, they sighted land. At first Ayres thought it was a cloud, but as they drew nearer he clearly saw a lighthouse. It was Lizard Lighthouse which was some 300 miles due east of the *Gairsoppa* sinking. They now headed towards a shore of high cliffs and crashing seas breaking fiercely on huge rocks. Ayres looked for a cove to land his ship. He finally sighted a cleft and shortened his sail to make a run for it.

As they neared the entrance to the cove, the turbulent seas threw the boat against the face of the cliffs. Caught by the backwash, the craft overturned, spilling the survivors into the churning sea. The Indians were trapped under the boat and drowned.

Ayres came to the surface and searched for his companions. Another wave pitched the boat upright and Ayres swam for it. Once in the boat he helped the gunner and radio operator climb aboard. Suddenly, another backwash cast them from the boat again. The three miraculously made it onto the keel, only to have a treacherous wave wash the radio officer off to his death.

Ayres and the gunner were swept off the bottom of the boat and each struck out for the gap leading to the cove. The gunner managed to reach the rocks and climb up one only to be hit by a sudden backwash and pitched to his death in the crashing sea.

Exhausted, Ayres was about to give up the struggle for his life when he heard the children's voices. Those voices of encouragement made him make one final, extraordinary effort. When brought ashore with the help of a young farmer who threw him a rope, Ayres was surrounded by some little girls who gave him some of their clothing to keep him warm until help arrived.

Ayres was taken to Helston hospital in Cornwall for recovery. The four little girls came to visit him within a few days and were certain that Ayres was not the man they had saved. That man had a beard. It didn't dawn on them that the patient had been shaved. Luckily for Ayres, the children were in the right place at the right time. They had been sent from Tottenham to Cornwall to escape the bombing of London.

After many months of care, Ayres recovered fully from his ordeal. He was subsequently made a Member of the Most Excellent Order of the British Empire. In announcing the award the *London Gazette* stated, "Undismayed by suffering and death, he had kept a stout heart and done all a man could do to comfort his shipmates and bring them to safety."[3]

Richard Ayres passed away in August of 1992. His family remembers that he made little mention of his experience over the years. He was much a fatalist in this respect, believing that "if one's number came up, that was it."[4]

CHAPTER TWO

133 DAYS ON A RAFT

The ship slowed in the late afternoon sun. The bridge hummed with activity as the watch carefully surveyed the surrounding waters. Was it a trick? Binoculars zeroed in on a lone man on a raft less than a mile ahead of them. German U-boats patrolling south Atlantic waters were known to use decoys to lure Allied shipping within attack range. Men along the rail of the ship and on its gun platform shaded their eyes as all attention was directed to the man frantically waving his arms toward them.

As they neared the raft they saw a slight, deeply bronzed man calling to them. Unfortunately, his words could not be heard across the water. "I from *Benlomond,* sink seven days. Help!" The man on the raft couldn't understand why the men on the ship delayed. Then he realized that he was being studied.

After a short time the ship's engines came to life and the bow swung away and headed on a course away from him. As it passed him he could clearly hear the pounding of the driving engines and the voices of men barking orders as the crew resumed its

Poon Lim, Chinese steward who survived 133 days on a raft in South Atlantic, August, 1943 - (U.S. National Archives)

shipboard routine. He was being abandoned. Deep in his heart Poon Lim knew the reason. They had deliberately left him because he was Chinese and not worth the risk.[5]

The British cargo ship *S.S. Benlomond* departed Capetown for Paramaribo, Dutch Guiana to pick up cargo on November 10, 1942. Thirteen days out and approximately 750 miles east of the Amazon River the ship was sighted by a patrolling German U-boat, *U-172*, under the command of Kapitänleutnant Carl Emmermann, a U-boat ace and winner of the Knight's Cross with Oak Leaves.

Emmermann sighted the steamer at dawn. He had a fine angle on the bow, just below the horizon. The seasoned commander steered his surfaced boat to the south just keeping his prey in sight. The *Benlomond* was making 13 knots and zigzagging every 10 minutes.

At 1334 the order, "Alarm!" rang throughout the U-boat and Emmermann took her down to attack depth. Thirty minutes later he was in position and fired torpedoes from tubes I and II. The first ran true and slammed into the steamer causing a powerful explosion. Watching the results of his first hit, Emmermann assumed a boiler explosion since a large cloud of steam began to rise from the ship. The second torpedo struck the fantail and another thunderous explosion rocked the ship. Two minutes later the *Benlomond* disappeared.

At the time of the attack, Poon Lim was about to leave his cabin to serve a light lunch. A sudden explosion toppled him to the deck and momentarily stunned him. As he got to his feet he could hear muffled cries of rushing crewmen, the wrenching sounds of cargo moving within the ship, and the hissing of steam below deck. A second explosion propelled him into the alley. Realizing that the ship was under attack, he raced back into his cabin, grabbed his life jacket and made for his abandon-ship station.

Fighting to keep his footing as the ship lurched and began to list, he reached the rail of his station only to find that his boat was gone. The steamer began to sink quickly by the stern. Poon, along with other crew members, jumped into the sea which was now turning black with oil that was oozing from the side of the ship.

As the ship slipped beneath the sea, Poon Lim was suddenly being sucked down in a dark swirl. Although he fought desperately to reach the fading light above, the watery funnel caused by the sinking ship took him deeper and deeper. Suddenly, he was thrust upward and burst to the surface, spitting, coughing, and vomiting. His kapok life jacket had saved his life.

Broken bodies in life jackets, shell cases, broken wooden spars, and all manner of debris filled the oil-drenched water around him. Not being a good swimmer, Poon looked for something to hang on to. He found a broken plank and clung to it while looking around for other survivors. He could hear the cries of other men somewhere in the wreckage.

Poon paddled further through the debris and caught sight of two men on a distant raft. He yelled and splashed the water around him trying to get their attention. Busy pulling a third man aboard their raft, they didn't hear or notice him. In panic, Poon thrust his plank aside and began swimming toward them in his life jacket. As he drew nearer, he called again but they didn't respond.

Weakening from his swim and vigorous efforts to signal the men on the raft, he grabbed a nearby wooden hatch cover to keep himself afloat. He continued to cough and spit up sea water darkened by spreading oil.

As he clung to the hatch, wondering what to do next, the sea suddenly opened and a U-boat conning tower and sliver-like deck appeared. Hatches clanged open and several men climbed out of the boat and raced to man fore and aft deck guns. Afraid of being sighted, Poon lowered himself deeper in the water.

A man in the conning tower shouted orders and the boat moved stern-first towards the men on the raft. U-boatmen reached across the water with long boat hooks and pulled the raft alongside. The survivors were ordered onto the boat where they climbed the ladder to the conning tower and disappeared below deck. Poon thought that there were four or five men.

The crewmen on the U-boat relaxed at their stations, chatting and lighting up cigarettes. Poon decided that his only chance for survival might lie with the enemy. He began shouting and waving at the men on the deck. "Help! Save me or I drown!" He plowed forward in the water towards the boat. One of the men at the aft gun station noticed him and turned to the others. They beckoned him on and he intensified his efforts to reach them.

Suddenly, the survivors of the *Benlomond* were on deck and being herded back onto their raft. The sub's engines roared to life and as Poon Lim waved and yelled frantically, the crewmen vanished from their deck positions, hatch covers closed and the U-boat submerged leaving him in its wake.

Emmermann recorded in his U-boat log that they had surfaced at 1445 and discovered from survivors that the ship was the *Benlomond*, 6,630 tons from Bombay, over Capetown, to a port of unknown destination to the survivors. *U-172* departed the area at 1454 for a new operational area.

Desolate now and fearful that his life would soon come to an end, Poon floated on the crest of swelling waves in the empty sea. He had lost track of time and his mind drifted to thoughts of his home and family back on Hainan Island. Suddenly, there was a glint of something ahead. Was the glaring sun playing tricks on him? Floating up and down in the troughs he caught momentary glimpses of the object. He swam towards it with all the strength he could muster. As he drew near he could clearly see that it was a raft, one of the ship's rafts. It was about 80 feet square, constructed of six watertight drums, framed by wooden planks with a platform and an open well. Fighting fatigue and a shifting sea, Poon managed to climb the 3 feet up to the platform where he collapsed and fell asleep.

The rocking motion of the raft awakened Poon and he slowly took stock of his situation. He pried open the drums and found that he had supplies for approximately 50 days if he was frugal. His stores included:

-Six boxes of hardtack

-Two pounds of chocolate

-Ten cans of pemmican (a concentrated preparation of dried beef, flour, molasses, and suet)
-One bottle of lime juice
-Five cans of evaporated milk
-Ten gallons of water

He also found four poles and a tarpaulin, a canvas piece to cover the well, some paddles, signal flares, smokepots, a can of massage oil, a flashlight, and some rope.

Poon was determined that he could and would survive. He was a young man in excellent physical condition. He was alone and thus could make his own decisions, and he decided never to give up! He reminded himself of the long struggles endured by his homeland in times of war and how China had survived against often impossible odds. He was suddenly heartened by the odds he felt were in his favor and set about surviving until help arrived.

As the days went by and Poon's supplies began to dwindle, he fashioned tools for fishing. The sea around him teemed with undersea life including sharks which now and then bumped against the raft.

He first made a small hook from the wire spring in his flashlight and baited it with pemmican which disintegrated when it hit the water. The hook was obviously inadequate to catch anything but small fish. He needed something bigger. Combing the raft's wooden planks, he found a nail deeply embedded in the wood. Pulling it out finally with his teeth, he hammered the nail into a reasonable-looking hook and tried it out without much success. However, his luck improved when he started using the small fish he caught with the smaller hook as bait. It was not long before he was pulling 20 pounders aboard. Poon would cut the fish and hang them in the sun to dry. When birds attempted to snatch the fish, he caught and ate them.

Early on in his ordeal, Poon had attached the tarpaulin to the four poles he found and lifted the canvas over the raft to provide shade and catch rain water for drinking. He fashioned one end lower than the other to let the water drain into a container.

On his one-hundredth day at sea, Poon sighted six planes on the horizon. Although they were flying high, he jumped to his feet and waved a flagged oar. He was overcome with joy as he waved and shouted when the aircraft turned towards him. The roar of their engines soon drowned his cries. Surely they must see him, he thought. But they flew on, dipping their wings towards the horizon. "Help! Come back! Help!" he shouted.

Suddenly, a plane broke from formation and flew directly towards him. Poon couldn't believe it. He had truly been seen. He laughed and cried as the silver winged aircraft began circling him at a low altitude and waggled its wings. Gaining altitude the plane dropped a smoke bomb which failed to ignite. It then climbed through high clouds and soon disappeared. Once again Poon had been found and left to die, or by some miracle, survive. He was devastated that the plane didn't land and pick him up, but finally rationalized to himself that the seas were too high for a safe landing. What he didn't know was that the aircraft did in fact report the sighting and position of Poon to the U.S. Naval authorities at Belem, Brazil. A rescue plane was dispatched to find Poon but was unable to locate him.

Finally, after a record 133 days at sea, Poon's raft was sighted by a Brazilian fishing boat 10 miles off the Brazilian coast east of Salinas. A man, a woman, and a girl looked across the water at a naked, wooly-haired man with skin darkened by oil and long exposure to the sun. They pulled alongside the raft and helped him into their boat. Although neither could speak the other's language, the Brazilians had no difficulty in understanding the plight of the man they had just pulled from the sea. Three days later they landed him at Belem. After 133 days adrift on a constantly moving platform, Poon, the lone survivor of the *Benlomond,* walked ashore under his own power.

The British Consul checked him into the Beneficiencia Portuguesa hospital in Belem where the nuns cared for him. It wasn't long before they delighted in the man whose personality warmed all who came in contact with him.

After 45 days of rest and recuperation, Poon was flown to New York via Miami to await transportation to England. While there he recounted his experience through interpreters to the Navy's Emergency Rescue Equipment Section in New York. He showed the group how he fashioned his fishing gear and other tools of survival. His raft was reconstructed and a film and photographs reenacting his experience were taken and used by Navy recruiting. Poon tried to join the U.S. Navy at the time but was rejected for having flat feet.

Poon was given several awards following his rescue. The British Colony in Belem presented him with a watch engraved with the words, "To Poon Lim, bravest of the brave." The War Shipping Administration by special order allowed Poon to wear the U.S. Merchant Marine Combat Bar with One Star, citing that, "His courage and fortitude will be an enduring inspiration to merchant seamen of all the United Nations." Next he was invested by King George VI with the British Empire Medal for "Display(ing) exceptional courage, fortitude, and resource in overcoming the tremendous difficulties with which he was faced during the long and dangerous voyage on a raft."

After the round of awards and notoriety came to an end, Poon wished to remain in the United States but was prohibited from immigrating by the 1882 Exclusion Law. In order to stay in America, the Chinese Consul obtained a "temporary visitor" visa for Poon. When the 1882 law was repealed in 1943, Poon still could not realize permanent status because of the very limited annual quota of 105 Chinese immigrants.

With the support of the Chinese Vice Consul, Poon was able to extend his stay in America by working as a parts inspector at the Wright Aeronautical Corporation in New Jersey until the war ended and then signing on as a messman for the United States Lines. In 1947, a special bill was introduced in the 81st Congress by Senator Warren G. Magnussen "To provide admission to, and the permanent residence in, the United States of Poon Lim." President Truman signed Private Law 178 on July 27, 1949 and Poon became a United States citizen in 1952.

That same year Poon Lim settled in Brooklyn, New York with his new bride. The matchmaker for the pairing was an old shipmate from the *S.S. Tanda*. Poon returned to the sea working with the United States Lines as Chief Steward until he retired in 1983. Poon Lim, perhaps the most extraordinary "sole survivor," has since passed away.

Poon's ordeal 50 years ago set a record for survival at sea which still stands today. The 1993 Guinness Book of Records lists Poon Lim's feat as follows: "Endurance and Endeavor: Longest on a raft. The longest recorded survival alone on a raft is 133 days (4 1/2 months) by Second Steward Poon Lim (b. Hong Kong) of Great Britain's Merchant Navy, whose ship, the *SS Benlomond* was torpedoed in the Atlantic 565 miles west of St. Paul's rocks at Lat. 00° 30′ N, Long. 38° 45′ W at 11:45 A.M. on 23 November 1942."[6]

CHAPTER

THREE

THE *DOGGERBANK* INCIDENT

Fritz Kuert, a German seaman during World War II, seemed to make it a habit of surviving misfortune at sea. In January of 1941, while serving aboard the *Freienfels* which was taking Axis troops from Tripoli to Bengasi, he managed to make it to a lifeboat and reach Liverno after the 12,000-ton freighter was torpedoed.[7]

Four months later he survived another sinking when his supply ship *Egina* was sent to the bottom by gunfire from British cruisers and destroyers as it made its way in convoy to Naples from Tripoli. Kuert was picked up by an Italian ship after swimming for 30 hours in the azure waters of the Mediterranean Sea.

Then in October of that same year, while on board the *Reichenfels,* he once again found himself treading water after the ship took direct hits from British bombers somewhere between the Libyan coast and Malta.

When Kuert finally ended his wartime adventures as the sole survivor of the German minelayer and supply ship *Doggerbank* in

On board the DOGGERBANK - *(Bibliothek für Zeitgeschichte Stuttgart)*

March of 1943, he found himself half way around the world talking to U.S. intelligence officers on the island of Aruba. His survival after 26 days at sea with practically no food or water was in itself a near miracle. However, his ordeal was so unique that the incident sparked some controversy in Germany following the war and generated articles and books to be written, some critical, about what happened during the days before he was rescued. Speculation still exists today.

Following the sinking of the *Reichenfels* and being rescued by an Italian destroyer, Kuert was taken to a hospital in Tripoli. After a brief recuperative period he was ordered to Brindisi and put aboard the 3,500-ton freighter *Sabona* which carried motor cars and tanks to Field Marshall Rommel's desert army.

Sabona was soon ordered to Banghazi under escort of an Italian destroyer. The two ships sailed to the west coast of Greece and while passing the port of Patrai were attacked by enemy bombers flying out of Malta. Although four planes were reportedly downed, the *Sabona* was seriously damaged and had to make Patrai for repairs. When the attack occurred most of the crew jumped overboard. The deck cargo of motor cars was destroyed and the ship's stack was damaged by one of the falling aircraft.

The ship returned to Brindisi following repairs and Kuert, unnerved at this point, went to see a doctor. On the verge of a breakdown, he made up his mind that he had made his last sea voyage. His requests for leave were denied and finally, after seeing another physician in Naples, he was granted 4 weeks leave to return to Germany. At the end of his leave period he was ordered to Hamburg, then sent to Madrid, and finally to Las Palmas where he was put aboard the 7,755-ton *Charlotte Schliemann*, a supply ship for German raiders and U-boats plying the South Atlantic and Indian Ocean.

The *Charlotte Schliemann* sailed from Las Palmas in February 1942, its destination unknown by the crew. After a day at sea the captain of the ship, Kapitän Rothe, called the crew together and informed them of their mission. Many of the crewmen, including Kuert, were disturbed to hear of their dangerous mission, this coming on top of their having been denied leave in Las Palmas. The ship carried no armament and hoisted no flag.

After 3 weeks time they met their first auxiliary cruiser, ''Ship 28'' (*Michel* under the command of Kapitän zur See Hellmuth von Ruckteschell) in the South Atlantic. After 6 hours of refuelling the raider, the two ships took leave of each other. The following April they met again and this time the cruiser transferred a number of prisoners from sunken ships to the *Schliemann*. The prisoners included American, British, and Chinese seamen.

According to Kuert, it was shortly after this, around April 16th, that the captain of the *Schliemann* called him into his cabin and notified him that he was being placed under arrest for possible sabotage. Evidently, the Chinese on board had overheard Kuert trying to make conversation with an American Boatswain and, hoping to gain favor with the captain, they informed him that the two were plotting a mutiny. Kuert was confined to his cabin under guard.

Later, the *Schliemann* joined up again with the *Michel* and the *Doggerbank*, a disguised minelayer and armed supply ship. Kuert was transferred to the auxiliary cruiser and after a review of his case by the skipper of the *Michel* he was found not guilty and released for transfer to the *Doggerbank*. The *Doggerbank* was the former British tramp ship, *Speybank*, which was captured by the German raider *Atlantis* in February 1941 in the Indian Ocean.[8]

Prior to Kuert's joining the crew of the *Doggerbank*, the vessel had laid mines off the coast of South Africa and then served as a supply ship in the South Atlantic. Under the command of Oberleutnant zur See Paul Schneidewind, the ship operated independently and was manned mostly by merchant seamen. After Kuert came aboard, the ship sailed for Japan where it took on mines, torpedoes, and other goods. She departed Kobe on December 17, 1942 and made for Saigon where she off loaded tobacco and took on a large cargo of sheet rubber. She next sailed for Singapore to top off her bunkers for the long voyage home but the needed oil was not available. Forced to refuel at Batavia, *Doggerbank* was finally ready to make her way across 10,000 miles of ocean water to Bordeaux.

To ensure safe passage for *Doggerbank* in the Atlantic, the German Naval War Staff (SKL) arranged with the Commander-in-Chief U-boats (B.d.U.) the establishment of an Atlantic "forbidden zone" in which U-boats would be forbidden to attack merchant ships between certain dates. The only problem was that the SKL couldn't know in advance what routes or shortcuts the *Doggerbank* might take to avoid the British blockade on its return trip. Schneidewind was provided with the latest intelligence on enemy activity along his route and given his "forbidden zone" time schedule before he sailed into the Indian Ocean.

Doggerbank reached the Atlantic and proceeded on track towards the "forbidden zone" without incident. Schneidewind had successfully avoided detection by altering his track and was thus ahead of schedule as he proceeded up the Canary Basin. He was faced with the choice of waiting west of the Canary Islands for his entry time into the zone or sailing onward, trusting that his luck would hold. He chose to press on.

On March 3, 1943 while approximately 1,000 miles west of the Canaries, a submarine was sighted about four miles off the port bow by a lookout in the crow's nest. The ship went to general quarters and all eyes strained to identify the distant vessel. It was decided that the submarine was a U-boat and the captain ordered that the recognition signal (a combination of colored hoses, pieces of sail cloth, flags, etc.) be hoisted. This was followed by the firing of Very pistol flares. By now the submarine had stopped and within minutes after the *Doggerbank* identified itself, the sub signalled a white light, the correct response. The crew on *Doggerbank* was overjoyed; they would soon be on dry land, see their families and friends, now that they were protected by their U-boats. What they didn't know was that the "forbidden zone" started on March 15th, 13 days later.

Thirty minutes later the *Doggerbank* was hit by three torpedoes. *U-43* under the command of Kapitänleutnant Hans Joachim Schwantke had fired on the ship believing it to be a British merchant ship, possibly the *Dunnottar Castle*. Ordered not to rescue survivors because of the *Laconia* incident (American planes had bombed three U-boats attempting to rescue British liner *Laconia* survivors), Schwantke left the scene and continued on patrol.

Schwantke's torpedoes proved fatal for *Doggerbank*. She had been hit in Nos. 1 and 3 holds and the engine-room. A hundred men lost their lives in the explosions. Within minutes the ship heeled to starboard and started sinking. Those caught below decks were doomed. Of the many above deck who were trying to escape the capsizing ship, only Kuert found a lifeboat of sorts. None of the six lifeboats on the *Doggerbank* were put overboard. What Kuert found was one of two Japanese small, flat-bottomed boats that had been brought aboard for painting the side of the ship in port. He cut the boat loose and jumped in along with the ship's dog, Leo.

That same evening Kuert hauled three other survivors aboard his flimsy craft, a boy named Waldemar Ring, Seaman Karl Boywitt, and Seaman Stachnovski. In bringing the men over the gunwale the boat began to fill with water. Fishing a 4-inch cartridge case out of the sea, the three men bailed water until the boat was out of danger of foundering. Kuert took stock of their situation. The boat had no mast, oars, food, or water, and they were at least 1,000 miles from the nearest landfall. Early the next morning Kuert and his mates picked up 11 other swimmers who were holding onto pieces of pressed rubber and floating debris from the ship. Among them was the captain, Paul Schneidewind.

The boat was now full to the point that any sudden movement might capsize the small craft. Three oars had been recovered from the sea and they were used to move the boat around the area in search of more survivors. It soon became apparent that they were the only survivors of the 150-man crew.

They next pulled a tarpaulin from the water and using the oars as a mast were able to rig a makeshift sail. Without a keel and overloaded, the flat-bottomed boat had no chance to make headway against the prevailing north-easterly tradewinds and reach land, perhaps the Canary Islands. They had little choice but to sail downwind towards South America some 1,500 miles away.

Although Schneidewind mentioned to the others that he thought they had been attacked by an American submarine, he probably knew in his own heart that his decision to press on before the "forbidden zone" went into effect cost him his ship and most likely the lives of his entire crew, including those around him.

As the days passed with no rescue in sight, the men weakened under the blazing sun. On March 14th during high winds and a swelling sea, the boat capsized and eight of the survivors and the ship's mascot, Leo, disappeared into the depths below. Unable to bail enough water out of the boat to right it and safely board it, the seven remaining men sat atop the craft as it wallowed in the sea. Giving up all hope, four of the survivors asked the captain to shoot them. Schneidewind took out his revolver and shot each of them in the temple. He then turned the gun on himself and dropped over the side.

With just two of them remaining, Kuert and the other survivor were able to right the boat, bail it out, climb back on board, and hoist the small sail. Kuert's companion lasted another week before he died and was put over the side. That same day, March 20th, a sudden rain shower gave Kuert some reprieve from his overwhelming thirst. His luck continued following the rains when a flying fish flopped into the boat. A second one found its way aboard the next day. These two fish were all that Kuert had to eat before his rescue a few days later.

On March 29th, 26 days after the *Doggerbank* was sunk, Kuert was picked up by the Spanish ship *Campoamor* which was outward bound from Barcelona to Aruba. Captain Joaquin de la Guerra, Master of the ship, pinpointed the rescue at 15.31 N, 51.25 W, about 500 miles from the nearest landfall. In his next daily position report to the Spanish Admiralty, Captain de la Guerra noted that he had rescued a survivor in a lifeboat at 1300 Peter and that the survivor would be disembarked upon arrival at Aruba. The message was intercepted by the U.S. Federal Communications Commission in San Juan, Puerto Rico, which in turn notified the Officer-in-Charge of the U.S. Intelligence Field Unit in Aruba.

The *Campoamor* arrived in Aruba on April 4th. Shortly after the ship had docked, Lieutenant T.B. Watkins, USNR, boarded the vessel and interviewed Captain de la Guerra.

The captain stated that the man was in very bad shape, near death when they picked him up. Since they had no doctor on board they communicated with another Spanish vessel, the *Cabo Buena Esperanza,* for advice as to treatment since he was under the impression that there was a doctor on board that ship. He was advised to give the man some brandy and other food. This was done and the survivor's recovery was remarkable. The captain noted that the response was so remarkable that it would be rather difficult for anyone to believe that the man had spent 26 days in an open boat on the high seas. He said that the lifeboat was in poor condition and that it was left adrift. He also stated that a terribly rusted automatic pistol was found in the boat and that he had personally thrown it into the sea. The survivor told him that he was from a German merchant ship called the *Doggerbank* which had been sunk by three torpedo hits. The torpedoing had taken place on March 3rd, late in the afternoon.

Lt. Watkins next went below decks to talk with the survivor. Kuert identified himself as a member of the German Merchant Marine who was born August 7, 1918 at Lunen, Germany. Watkins reported the survivor as having blond hair, blue eyes, 5′6″ tall, and two gold teeth in the front lower jaw. Additionally, he had tattooed on his left arm the Danish flag and various other figures. On his right arm was a boxer and a girl.

Watkins took custody of the prisoner and escorted him to the intelligence office for more questioning. Later, he was released to the Dutch police for custody and then transferred to the U.S. Army hospital at Camp Savaneta for a complete physical checkup. While at the hospital, Kuert was interviewed extensively by a group of Allied intelligence officers.

One discrepancy in Kuert's story bothered the intelligence officials and that concerned the gun the captain of the *Campoamor* said he found in the boat. Kuert was informed of the captain's statement and he insisted that it was not true and said that Captain Schneidewind went to his death with his gun clutched tightly in his hand. He further stated that the morning after the torpedoing they picked up a board or two floating in the water and used them to hang up the captain's watch and his pistol holster. He also mentioned that the holster was in the boat, but there was no pistol when he was rescued. Finally, Kuert said that he distinctly remembered that when the captain shot the crew members, he pulled the gun from under his coat.

Unfortunately, *Campoamor* departed Aruba while Kuert was being questioned; thus, it was impossible to further interrogate the master of the ship about the revolver in question and its holster.

Kuert was subsequently transferred to the United States and further interrogated. He was sent to a POW camp where he remained until the end of the war at which time he was repatriated back to Germany. However, controversy about Kuert's tale of survival continued in Germany after the war.

One author wrote that, "His tale was that of a madman, as he accused himself, out of pure selfishness, of having shot his comrades in the lifeboat, including the captain whose pistol he had stolen during the night." This statement, if it in fact was ever made by Kuert, was at odds with the account he gave to the Allied intelligence authorities and in an article he wrote many years later for the German magazine *Das Grune Blatt*. Though certain details varied between his interrogation and his written article, he remained consistent in one detail, that Captain Schneidewind committed suicide. This has been questioned by the family, relatives, and friends of the Captain who refused to believe that the strongly-willed Schneidewind would take his own life. However, in a seemingly hopeless situation such as the that in which the *Doggerbank* survivors found themselves, who could possibly know what one might do.

Only Fritz Kuert knows what happened on that tiny harbor boat out in the Mid Atlantic those many years ago. He has stuck to his story through the years and thus his sole survivor account closes the book forever on *Doggerbank* and her ill-fated ending.

CHAPTER FOUR

BLACK FRIDAY

Shortly after midnight on October 20, 1916, the whaleback steamer *James B. Colgate* departed Buffalo Harbor for Fort William, Ontario. Loaded with coal, the 50-foot, steel hulled Lake freighter made its way past the harbor's breakwater and out into the open waters of Lake Erie where a rising wind and rolling seas began to hammer the 3,300 ton fully loaded vessel.[9]

A storm warning had been sent out by the Weather Bureau at Buffalo but there was never a thought of turning back by the 40-year-old skipper of the *Colgate,* Captain Walter Grashaw. The 24-year-old freighter had made its way through many fierce storms on the Great Lakes and Captain Grashaw, standing at the ship's wheel in oilskins and sou'wester, wasn't the kind of seaman to let a bit of a blow stay his journey. Having sailed the Lakes since he was 14, Grashaw had served as the *Colgate* 's first mate for 10 years before being given command of the ship just 2 weeks before this sailing. He was confident of his boat and crew of 23. He had a cargo to deliver.

Whaleback JAMES B. COLGATE - (The Great Lakes Historical Society)

Colgate made slow headway during the night hours as it bucked heavy seas. At dawn she had made it to Long Point on the Canadian shore just opposite Erie, Pennsylvania. The larger, open waters of the Lake lay ahead. Squall winds shrieked out of the southwest under leaden skies. Unaware, Captain Grashaw was about to take his ship into one of the worst storms in Great Lakes' history. That day in October was to be known forevermore as "Black Friday." Captain Grashaw recalled that:

"Foul weather struck us in earnest with the dawn. All of that day we fought the mounting waves, and by nightfall we struck a gale of seventy-five miles an hour from the southwest. There was little any of us could do. We were making slight headway; but we could keep the engines going, confident that we could weather the storm.

"Confidence was the note that ran around the table as we messed that night. Then the crew gathered aft to sing and wait for the wind to blow itself out. 'She's listing!' came a shout at eight o'clock. The seas were rolling over us, washing the deck from bow to stern. Clinging to every support, I made my way through the wall of water to the bridge. As each wave struck, the vessel shivered. And the wind howled. I played the searchlight forward over the deck hoping to make out the cause of the listing that now had all the crew alarmed.

"The searchlight sent a shaft of white light through the murky night, and where it fell upon the hatches I could see them rising and falling, as the water dashed around the hold. Not a man could have gone forward to investigate. I left the searchlight pointed straight up in the hope that it might be seen as a signal of our distress. Then I went to rejoin the crew.

"Above the fury of the storm, I caught snatches of prayer. 'Oh God, remember my three little babies at home.'Another man spoke of his mother. Prayers, curses, imprecations, mingled in a frenzied clamor to which the waves smashing down on us, and the howling wind played a crashing and shrieking obbligato.

"The boats and life rafts were made ready, and then the *Colgate* simply dropped away from under us. What happened to the twenty-three others I do not know. What happened to the boats, I do not know. For a long time, I struggled deep in the icy water. When I came up in the pitch blackness of the night I sighted the Coston light on a raft, swam to it and drew myself up on it. The raft although five feet wide by nine feet long, bobbed like a sliver of wood at the mercy of the waves. Gradually, I became conscious of two other objects on the raft with me. I recognized one as Harvey Ossman, second engineer. The other was a man, a coal passer, I could not remember having seen before, but the night was too black, even at that close range, to make out his features.

"Slowly, we hunched over the center of the raft, and lay there, face downward. On the crest of the waves we rose eighteen or twenty feet and then dropped back with breath-taking suddenness.

"We had been there about three hours, I think, when the raft rolled completely over. I regained it by supreme effort, and reached a hand to Ossman, pulling him back onto the raft. We strained our eyes for some glimpse of our unknown comrade. His head did not appear above the surface and we did not see him again.

"My clothes seemed to be freezing on me. My legs began to swell and I ached in every joint. Through the night we clung face down to the raft, shifting with the dizzy rising and falling, hoping to keep it righted. Ossman was apparently all in. He lay so still I thought he was dead. I urged him to kick his legs to keep up the circulation, but he was so weak he could not. Once more the raft went completely over, again I grabbed it as I came up and crawled on. Ossman rose to the surface, battling weakly. I caught him by the coat and pulled him over toward the raft.I got him half on, and he lay there several minutes, nearly dead. Eventually, I got him entirely on, but he could not move.

"The fury of the storm was abating little by little, but the waves were still whipping the raft around, and in the midst of this vast expanse of seething water what might happen to me seemed of little consequence. I debated with myself whether I might go, or keep up the fight.

"Toward dawn of Saturday, the raft again rolled over, I felt myself going down, and in a flash I thought death would be welcome. For a second, I gave up the struggle. And then, the thought of my wife and babies at home swept over me and half consciously I renewed the fight with the last ounce of my energy. I came up and by some miracle reached the raft; Ossman was gone.

"I lay there for hours that seemed an eternity. Once more, I remembered my aching legs and began to kick about. As daylight came I discovered to my unutterable happiness that the storm was nearly over. I could then, by a great effort, sit up on the raft, move my arms and shout.

"Through the night only death seemed my fate. Now hope returned. Far off on the horizon, I saw a streak of smoke. In a frenzy, I renewed my shouting and wild throwing of my arms. Nearer and nearer came the smoke. The stacks and then the hull of a boat came into view, bearing down on me. I knew it was the Buffalo boat, and I wept in my joy. Two puffs came from the steamer's whistle, but I could not hear the blasts, but I knew that I had been seen. Then, suddenly the steamer altered her course, steamed by, and left me there, as I thought, to die.

"Again I lay flat, cursing the heartless Captain. Once more, I sat painfully erect, looking around, and there, not two hundred feet back of me came the *Marquette &*

> *Bessemer Car Ferry, No.* 2. This was the explanation of the Buffalo boat passing by. Her master had seen the car ferry much closer to me, had signalled her, and gone on."[10]

A boat was lowered from the car ferry and Captain Grashaw was lifted onto the deck of the ferry. He had been on the raft, adrift, for almost 35 hours.

Once aboard the ferry, he vaguely remembered being put to bed, and later being landed at Conneaut and taken to Grace Hospital where he spent a week recovering from his ordeal. A physician at the hospital stated that Captain Grashaw would never have survived his battle against the elements had he not been such a healthy and clean-minded man. "Had he been a man dependent on stimulants," said the physician, "given to intoxicants instead of never touching them, or given to the use of tobacco thereby weakening his heart action, he would not have had the physical strength to endure. It took every ounce of his 200 pounds, every inch of his six feet to make the fight."

Four vessels were lost on Lake Erie that "Black Friday." Fifty-two seamen died and property loss was set at $500,000.

Following his shipwreck, Captain Grashaw served as mate on the *Dawson* and master of the *Progress*. For many years the *Progress* with Captain Grashaw on the bridge was the first ship to open spring navigation on Lake Erie. That first trip from Detroit to Cleveland was usually made in March.

Captain Grashaw died on January 22, 1928. His survivors included his wife, Flora, two sons, Nelson and J. Walter, and a daughter, Marjorie Clair.

Nelson sailed with his father for several years and considered him to be one of the bravest, strictest, most considerate men he ever knew. His father never talked much about the shipwreck. He did say that the waves were as high as a house and most houses in those days were 35 to 40 feet high. He also felt that if Harvey Ossman didn't smoke cigarettes he probably would have made it.[11]

CHAPTER FIVE

OPERATION ICEBERG

In the late spring of 1945, U.S. Pacific invasion forces zeroed in on the 60 mile long island of Okinawa in the Ryukyu group south of Formosa. Once secured, the island could be used to tighten the blockade around the enemy homeland and act as a staging base for American bombers striking Japan's major cities. This was to be the last American amphibious operation of the war.[12]

Tabbed ''Operation Iceberg,'' the Okinawa expeditionary forces employed the largest fleet ever to assemble in naval history. Over 40 aircraft carriers, 18 battleships, scores of cruisers, submarines, minesweepers, landing craft, patrol vessels, salvage ships, and auxiliaries. Approximately 150 destroyers and destroyer-escorts included in the armada bore the brunt of the sea-air battle with extraordinary bravery typical of their wartime tradition.[13]

Commencing with the initial assault on Easter Sunday, April 1, the two and a half month campaign proved to be the most costly operation for naval forces during the entire war. Thirty-four ships and support craft were lost and 386 damaged. Some 5,000 navymen were killed and another 4,824 wounded. Most of the casualties were due to devastating kamikaze air strikes which caused targets to become blazing infernos when struck.

The 77,000 defenders of the island under the command of Lieutenant General Mitsuru Ushijima were finally overcome on June 21. The American Tenth Army, 183,000 strong, which was comprised of the 1st, 2nd, and 4th Marine Divisions and four army infantry divisions, lost 7,613 killed and 31,800 wounded.[14]

As American invasion forces moved into position off the island during the end of March, naval gunners and carrier pilots fought off enemy bombers and suicide planes. Several Japanese submarines prowled the waters off the island. However, they were not a factor in the campaign and all were sunk by U.S. destroyers to the east and southeast of the island.

One boat ordered to Okinawa was I-8 under the command of Lieutenant Commander Shigeo Shinohara. At one time during the war the submarine was commanded by Captain Tatsunosuke Ariizumi, infamous for his brutal treatment of Allied seamen. On March 26, 1944 he killed 98 survivors of the Dutch merchant ship *Tjisalak*. A month later 96 survivors of the American steamer, *Jean Nicolet*, who had been picked up by the *I-8*, were wounded by being forced to run through a gauntlet of the crew. Twenty-three eventually survived after the submarine dived leaving the bound and wounded seamen on deck. Ariizumi committed suicide when his last command, the *I-400*, was about to be taken over by the U.S. Navy in August 1945.[15]

During the late evening hours of March 30, *I-8* was detected by the destroyer *U.S.S. Stockton* (DD646). *Stockton* was a member of a four-ship task unit which was enroute to Kerama Retto. At 2308 the destroyer picked up the sub on its radar at 12,800 yards. During the next two hours *Stockton* carried out eight depth charge attacks on the elusive enemy. The crew detected the smell of oil in the air as they strove to make the kill. Either they had seriously injured their prey or the oil had been released from the submerged boat as a ruse to ward off further attack.

At 2345 the *U.S.S. Morrison* (DD560) was ordered to relieve the *Stockton*. The *Morrison* arrived on scene at 0235 and together with an antisubmarine patrol bomber, which periodically illuminated the surface, continued to track the submarine. The action report of the *Morrison* details the subsequent action and destruction of the *I-8*[16].

> "At 0302 the MORRISON gained sound contact bearing 298 degrees True, range 500 yards, and proceeded to make an attack. Due to the short range of the initial contact, insufficient bearings and ranges were received to insure a good attack course, so no charges were dropped. Contact was lost at fifty yards, indicating the submarine was at very shallow depth. At 0310 contact was regained, but contact proved to be a wake. At 0324 contact was regained in search sector recommended by Combat Information Center (C.I.C.), and a deliberate attack was started. C.I.C. plot, doppler and range rate showed a deep quarter track. At 0330.5 an eleven-charge pattern was dropped with a shallow setting. Submarine at this time was turning to starboard. Range was being opened for another attack when the sound operator, SUACCI, Eugene V., 378 29 17, SoM2c, V-6, USNR, announced that he had heard definite accelerated propeller noises and, also, the submarine's tanks being blown, indicating that the submarine was surfacing. Submarine surfaced at a 45 degree angle on starboard bow, distance 900 yards, and was immediately taken under fire by 20MM, 40MM and 5"/38 caliber battery. MORRISON attempted to ram submarine by coming hard right, but submarine was turning hard right towards the ship, apparently trying to bring its forward tubes to bear. Due to the relatively short range, the attempt to ram the sub was unsuccessful. Morrison passed down submarine's starboard side, astern, and up its portside, keeping it under fire. At 0338 we fired three starboard "K" guns at shallow setting. Range to submarine at this time was 200 yards. The deck gun on

the sub was not manned at any time during the action, due to the consistent coverage of the topside by the 20MM and 40MM guns. Many hits were also registered on the conning tower and entire hull by the 5''/38 caliber battery, and a large explosion was observed.

''At 0340 we came left and circled to open range to be clear of forward tubes and be able to ram sub. At 0351 submarine submerged except for its bow and conning tower, so we did not ram for fear of damaging our propellers and passed astern of sub. The sub then fully surfaced on even trim, and it was kept under continuous fire by the MORRISON.

''After surfacing the submarine was tracked by the Mark 12-22 fire control radar until it was dead in the water at 0340. At 0412 submarine sank, stern first, in 2800 fathoms of water at latitude 25 degrees 29 minutes N and Longitude 128 degrees 35 minutes E. MORRISON commenced Operation Observant to await sunrise for further evaluation and confirmation of sinking. At 0636 one live survivor was sighted off port bow in considerable debris which included deck planking, dry stores, rolls of toilet tissue and mangled bodies. Japanese survivor was recovered by boat and given medical treatment for multiple shrapnel wounds. Survivor appeared to be in excellent physical condition and was later placed in custody of Commander Western Islands Attack Group (CTG 51.1) for interrogation. When asked by the interpreter what the name of the submarine was, he replied, 'If your ship were sunk, would you release the name?' Fifteen eye-witnesses who were in good position to see the submarine the entire thirty-seven minutes it was surfaced identified it as an I-5 Class.''

Although no CTG 51.1 records regarding interrogation of the lone survivor of I-8 could be located, a personal account of the survivor's experience was found in a journal written by the former Submarine Commanding Officer of the Imperial Japanese Navy, Mochitsura Hashimoto.

"At about 10.30 p.m. on March 30 the look-out sighted an approaching enemy destroyer and I.8 immediately crash-dived and received her first depth-charge attack at a depth of about ninety feet. She was then continuously attacked for four hours until she eventually sank. The attacks were accurate, as the enemy was easily able to determine our position by the sound of our propellers. As the attacks increased in intensity, the crew's quarters aft were holed and the compartment started to flood. We did our best to effect repairs, but it was of little avail, and the boat went down to four hundred and fifty feet, with the bow inclining upwards at an angle of twenty-five degrees, causing the bilge water to surge aft. The boat continued to sink. Something had to be done and the captain gave the order to blow the after tanks. This made bubbles rise to the surface, causing a white patch which provided an excellent target for the attackers. We stood by awaiting death. All our torpedoes were gone and the captain decided to surface and try to fight it out with the gun. Orders were given to blow the main ballast tanks. All power in the boat was already stopped. It was 2 a.m. on March 31. I was one of the gun's crew, standing by in the conning-tower while the boat surfaced at an angle of twenty degrees. The hatches were opened and we emerged. There was a destroyer to starboard and we engaged it with the 25-mm machine gun. Two of us manned the 14-cm gun and had just got it loaded when I was wounded in the foot by a shell splinter. I tried to get on to the bridge but at that moment it was blown apart, leaving a large gaping hole. I was just trying to get back to the gun when I sighted an enemy cruiser. Attacked by two enemy warships at a range of about three thousand yards, I.8 hadn't the slightest chance. Soon she turned over and sank. It was by this time 2.30 a.m. I was in great pain, but managed to keep afloat. There was one other person floating, but I didn't know who it was. There was plenty of wind with a big swell and pale moonlight. After what seemed like about two hours I came to in the sick bay of the U.S. destroyer."[17]

CHAPTER

SIX

THE *HENRY STANLEY*

Richard Jones was born in 1885 and, like many youngsters of the time, he used to hang around the old harbor in Amlwch, a coastal town in Northern Wales. He spent his time with his young mates watching the ships and sloops sailing in and out of the harbor and talking to sailors about exotic lands far across the sea.[18]

At the age of 16 he made his first voyage as a cook on board the *Irish Minstrel*. A year later he signed on aboard the three-masted schooner *John Lockett* of Liverpool for a voyage to Cape Town. After discharging their cargo of coal, the ship sailed for Sydney, Australia where Jones and a few of his shipmates decided to leave the ship and explore the rather primitive country.

After 8 months of working at various jobs on sheep farms, Jones realized that if he wished to become a true seaman he would need education. Returning to Amlwch, he attended evening navigation classes. Soon thereafter he gained his second mate's certificate and joined the Elder Dempster Lines of Liverpool in 1912. Five years later, after serving on various ships of

Captain Richard Jones - (Mr. Emrys Jones)

the company, he acquired his master's certificate. After serving as chief officer in many ships, he was appointed to his first command on the *SS New Brooklyn* in January of 1935.

When war erupted, Captain Jones was skipper of the *SS David Livingston*, then the *SS Edward Blyden*. His next command was the *MS Dixcove*, a 3,790-ton single screw motorship which departed London on June 14, 1941 for discharge of general cargo at various West African ports. On her return trip home she joined a convoy (SL.87, Freetown to England). The convoy consisted of 13 merchant vessels in five columns of two and one column of three vessels. Although protected by five escorts, seven merchant ships were lost to enemy U-boats. Among them was the *Dixcove*.

At 0430 GMT on Wednesday, September 24 at a position about 350 miles west of the Madeira Islands, the *Dixcove* was struck by a torpedo which caused a tremendous explosion aboard ship. At the time of the attack, Captain Jones was approaching the companion ladder outside his cabin. The impact of the explosion caused him to be thrown down hard against the ladder, badly injuring one of his legs.

Lifeboats were lowered into the water as the ship began to slowly sink by the head. Captain Jones was assisted into one of the boats. By 0900 hours GMT, the convoy had circled round to pick up the survivors who were subsequently transported to Belfast where Captain Jones was admitted to a hospital.

SL.87 had run into a wolfpack of U-boats, five of which shared in the sinking of seven merchantmen, e.g., *U-68* (Merten), *U-562* (Hamm), *U-103* (Winter), *U-67* (Muller-Stockheim) and *U-107* (Hessler), which sunk the *Dixcove* and two other ships.[19]

Eight months later, Captain Jones was at sea again commanding his old ship the *David Livingston*. He next transferred to the *Henry Stanley* where he survived a second U-boat sinking, only this time he was the sole survivor.

The *Henry Stanley* sailed from Liverpool on November 28, 1942 with 60 crewmen and 12 passengers, after loading a full cargo of general merchandise totalling approximately 4,000 tons. Included in the cargo was about 15 tons of gelignite which was stowed in No. 3 hold. She joined a 45-ship convoy (ON.149d, U.K. to Freetown) and was allocated No. 74 Position.

On December 5th, the ship was well into the Atlantic when orders were received for the convoy to disperse and proceed independently without escort to Freetown. On the following day, at 1000 hours, Captain Jones received a warning by radio that U-boats were in the area. The vessel commenced a zig-zag course during the day and carried out evasive steering during the night. Weather conditions during the night were a light westerly wind, heavy swell, fine and clear. A speed of about 12 knots was maintained, and the passage was uneventful until 1145 hours on December 7th when the ship was approximately 580 miles west of the Azores Islands.

Captain Jones was standing on the monkey bridge island with Captain Brown of the Blue Funnel Line, who was travelling to Freetown as a passenger, when an explosion occurred on the starboard side forward in way of No. 1 hold well under the waterline. It was apparent that the *Henry Stanley* had been struck by a torpedo. However, neither the torpedo nor the submarine was seen by any of the lookouts. Engines were immediately stopped, and the third officer (S.J. Williams) in the meantime blew the whistle for emergency boat stations. All crew and passengers assembled at their respective stations in a very orderly fashion. The vessel was, by this time, beginning to settle by the head.

Captain Jones, anticipating that his vessel would soon be hit by a second torpedo, immediately ordered "abandon ship." Some of the passengers and crew entered the four lifeboats at the boat deck and were lowered into the water, and the remainder went down the Jacob's ladder. Approximately 10 minutes after the explosion, all four lifeboats had pulled away from the ship and stood off at a safe distance.

After waiting for about 30 minutes, Captain Jones intended to instruct all lifeboats to return to the ship, when suddenly she was struck by a second torpedo in way of No. 3 hatch. A tremendous explosion occurred and all concluded that this second attack had detonated the gelignite, stowed in the hatch. Forty-five seconds later, the *Henry Stanley* disappeared beneath the sea.

With a heavy swell rolling, and rescue improbable, Captain Jones decided to gather his lifeboats together and set course for Fayol in the Azores some 500 miles to the east. Given favorable weather he estimated that they could have made the journey in 7 days' time.

Within a few hours *U-103*, under the command of Kapitänleutnant Gustav-Adolf Janssen, surfaced and came up to within 30 feet of the lifeboats.

Janssen called out, "Is the Captain there?"

Captain Jones answered, "Yes!"

He was then ordered to bring his lifeboat alongside the U-boat and embark. Among the occupants of lifeboat No. 2 was Commander Cadiz, R.N., Captain Brown, and Major Law (all passengers). Captain Jones was afraid that if such persons were seen, particularly Commander Cadiz who was in uniform, they would be taken prisoner. He therefore replied, "I won't bring my boat alongside as I feel it is far too dangerous owing to the heavy swell running. My boat might be damaged and made useless for the crew."

The U-boat commander gave Captain Jones a very quick and curt reply, "I don't care a damn about your crew."

Captain Jones then took off his bridge coat and mackintosh, passed them and command to Captain Brown. He jumped into the water and swam towards the U-boat, was hauled on board and quickly hurried below where he was given some dry clothes.

"The war is finished for you; I am taking you to Germany," said Janssen. Captain Jones replied, "I am your prisoner today, but you may be mine tomorrow."

Jones was then questioned as to the name of his ship, what cargo she was carrying and her destination. Captain Jones informed his interrogators that he was bound for Freetown from Liverpool with a general cargo. Janssen replied, "You had something more than general cargo aboard your ship," and did not believe that the *Henry Stanley* was bound from Liverpool to Freetown owing to her position and suggested that she was in fact bound from Halifax, Canada, to a port in North Africa.

Later a gale blew up from the West and at about 1800 hours the commander asked Captain Jones to accompany him to the conning tower, as he proposed to look for the lifeboats and offer assistance where possible. On reaching the conning tower the weather was extremely bad. The boat was turned about and ran before the wind and sea towards a position where the lifeboats were expected to be. Only the faint sound of their motors could be heard in the distance. Later the emergency radio set of one of them could be heard on the U-boat's receivers, vainly trying to contact England.

Amidst fierce gales and heavy snow squalls, Janssen decided to pursue the lifeboats to see if they needed assistance. However, while plowing through the deepening troughs, the U-boat shipped a very heavy sea over the stern which flooded the engine room to a depth of 18 inches. Janssen quickly abandoned the search and promptly submerged. The severe gale continued for about three days and nights. During that time the U-boat remained submerged during the day and surfaced at night to recharge its batteries.

On December 19th, Janssen called Captain Jones to the conning tower to observe nine other boats alongside the *U-103* in a line abreast formation. They were bound for a mid-Atlantic rendezvous with a "Milchkuh," a Type XIV U-boat tanker that carried stores, petrol supplies, lubricating oil, food, fresh fruit and vegetables, and even a doctor, who went on board each U-boat to tend to German crewmen.

Captain Jones watched as the tanker refuelled four U-boats at a time by means of rubber hoses, reinforced and buoyed while all the vessels remained on course. Replenishment operations were completed in 3 hours and the sea was once again clear as the boats submerged and headed for their patrol areas.

Reaching the end of its patrol, *U-103* headed for its home base at Lorient, arriving there on December 31, 1942. Captain Jones was landed and sent on a 48-hour train trip to a Wilhelmshaven interrogation camp along with three other ship masters and 40 coolies. There he was relieved of all his papers and subjected to further interrogation. Black bread and water was the staple there, with execrable coffee and cabbage leaf soup as highlights of the menus. He was placed in solitary confinement which lasted for about 17 days, after which he was moved to Milag Nord prison camp. Captain Jones was eventually repatriated by the British Army on April 26, 1945 as the Allies swept through Europe. He and four other Welsh ship masters were given a real Welsh welcome by the men of the Welsh Guards armored unit which captured the camp.

No further news was ever heard of the passengers and crew that remained in the lifeboats from the *Henry Stanley* and it can only be assumed that they were all lost during the heavy gale which followed the sinking.

Captain Jones returned to the sea in late 1945, taking command of the *Deido*. He retired several years later to his home in Amlwch where he died in 1961.

CHAPTER SEVEN

SAPPER ERIC MUNDAY ROYAL ENGINEERS

In November 1942, the 18,713-ton British passenger liner *Ceramic* left Liverpool, England with convoy ON.149. The 30-year-old ship built for the Shaw, Savill and Albion Line had for many years sailed between England and Australia, carrying passengers and cargo. On this voyage she carried a crew of 278, including 14 D.E.M.S. gunners (armed guards named after the Defensively Equipped Merchant Ship Program), 378 passengers, naval and military personnel, and women and children. Her cargo consisted of 12,362 tons of general and government stores. Among her passengers was Sapper Eric Munday, Royal Engineers. He was to be her sole survivor on the ill fated journey.[20]

Ceramic was to sail with the convoy to a point off Greenland and then proceed independently to St. Helena, Durban, and Sydney. Although the threat of U-boat attack was ever present on such a long journey, the ship had been lucky. It had safely made the round trip up to now without incident, thanks, perhaps, to its 17 knot cruising speed. She could give an attacking U-boat a

CERAMIC at Cape Town in the late 1930's - (National Maritime Museum)

run for its money and under the right conditions could outrun her adversary.

As the ship left the convoy and set course southward, the weather was clear and the seas calm. Sapper Munday remembered their detachment from the convoy on the second or third of December and their proceeding independently.

However, off to the west a lone surfaced German U-boat had sighted the masts of the liner approximately 16 miles to the east and proceeded to stalk its prey. *U-515*, under the command of Kapitänleutnant Werner Henke, holder of the Knight's Cross with Oak Leaves, had only recently been ordered away from the Gibraltar area to converge on convoys further out to sea. Admiral Dönitz, Supreme Commander U-Boats, had suffered too many losses in the close-in sea routes leading to the coast of North Africa and the Mediterranean. He thus directed Henke's wolf-pack to patrol West of the Azores.

Henke's log book described the U-boat's intercept of the liner and his attack on an unsuspecting enemy.[21]

6.12

1600 2 smoke clouds in sight, true 220 degrees, 7000 tons freighter, true 70 degrees a large four masted passenger vessel. I am drawing ahead of four-master. At dawn vessel increases speed now to 17 knots. Only after hours-long full speed I am finally getting ahead.

2359 *Double shot tubes I and IV*, depth 5, speed 15.5, bow right bearing 80, distance 1200, running time 30 seconds. Hitting mid-engine room. 2nd shot, hearing impact, apparently pistol failure. Vessel using radio. It is the *Ceramic*, 18,800 GRT.

Sapper Munday recalled that the ship was hit by a torpedo forward on the starboard side. Although the weather was fairly calm, it was very dark with poor visibility. The vessel took a list, but her speed did not lessen as the engines were not damaged.

Twenty minutes later Henke attacked again.

7.12

0018 *Catch shot tube V*, depth 3, hitting forward 20, illuminating vessel which is setting out lifeboats. I can see at close range several boats with soldiers in them.

0038 *Catch shot tube VI,* depth 4, hitting aft 40, vessel does not sink, many floats and boats are being set out.

Almost immediately after the first torpedo crashed into the ship, "action stations" was sounded. After the first explosion the *Ceramic* was struck simultaneously by two torpedoes amidships and the order was given to abandon ship. Munday recalled that all three explosions were dull, no columns of water were thrown up and he estimated that the torpedo hits were deep since there was no visible damage on deck. At the time of the attack he was in the lounge and quickly made his way to his boat station on the port side. He remembered some panic, probably owing to having women and children on board, but he considered it nothing serious and quite understandable as it was so very dark that some confusion was inevitable."I do not know what happened on the starboard side, but probably the starboard boats were damaged, as there were many more people in my boat than were allocated to it, probably many people came over to the first boat they could find. The boat was lowered successfully, however, and we managed to get away from the ship's side after a struggle."

Soon Henke sent another torpedo into the doomed ship.

0100 *Catch shot tube II,* depth 6, hitting forward 20, vessel is breaking up, sinking after 10 seconds. Suddenly there is a very strong detonation near to me, I am distancing myself fearing defense.

Six or eight boats were able to get away from the sinking vessel along with numerous rafts. Munday recalled.

> "We lay to for the rest of the night, keeping the boat head to sea, as it was too crowded to move about in the darkness, also as there were mostly military personnel in the boat nobody knew very much about handling it. By daylight a northerly gale had sprung up, with storms of rain and sleet, with high confused seas. Huge waves were breaking over the boat, we bailed furiously, but it was impossible to free the boat of water before another wave crashed over, swamping it so that it capsized and we were all thrown into the water. After a

> struggle the boat was righted, but it was three-quarters full of water; two or three men climbed in and tried to bail it out, but again it was capsized by the huge waves. It was then about 0800 on the 7th, and I decided to swim off. I found some wreckage and clung to that for a little while, but the seas were too strong and it was washed away."

In the meantime Henke had been ordered back into the area to gather intelligence about the ship. Headquarters wanted to know the ship's destination and the mission of its large military contingent.

1200 Position 41.17 N/41.06 W, wind SSW7, increasing, westerly swell, overcast, cloudy 10 vis. 3-4 sm, hail showers. Approaching again location of vessel sunk in order to take the Captain prisoner. At the location where the ship sank there were many dead army and naval soldiers, about 60 floats and many boats and parts of planes. According to reports of survivors there had been on board 45 officers, about 100 ratings. Nothing could be found out about destination and cargo. I suspect that the cargo consisted exclusively of war materials. Submerged account weather condition.

What Henke failed to mention in his official log was the retrieval of Sapper Munday, the eventual sole survivor of the *Ceramic*.

> "About four hours after swimming away from the boat, at noon on the 7th December, I was picked up by the submarine. She had surfaced to look for the Captain, but being unsuccessful, and seeing me nearby in the water, I was hauled on board. I do not know the number of the U-boat but I believe the Captain was a Lieutenant Commander named Henke. I did not actually hear his name mentioned whilst I was on board. I was treated well on the whole; several of the crew could speak English fairly well, in particular a young Midshipman, who told me that a number of boats and rafts were seen to leave the ship and that the vessel took

about 3 hours to sink. I am of the opinion that the weather was so bad when the storm blew up during the early hours of the 7th December, that no boat could have survived, and this accounts for the great loss of life.

"The German midshipman told me that about a fortnight before the *Ceramic* was sunk, the U-boat had torpedoed a British cruiser. A destroyer had come to the rescue of her crew, and whilst survivors were being picked up the submarine torpedoed her also. I heard no other reports of any merchant ships being sunk by the submarine on this cruise, which had lasted about a month when the *Ceramic* was sunk.

"We arrived at Lorient on the 6th January, 1943 in company with a Flotilla of U-boats. During the return voyage to that port we were attacked once by Sunderland flying-boats but no damage was sustained. On arriving at Lorient I met several Army and Air Force Officers, and a Merchant Captain, from other ships, all of whom had been picked up by other U-boats. We were asked if we would like to give our names and addresses, together with the name of our respective ships, so that this information could be broadcast and our relatives thus learn that we were safe.

"We all agreed to do this; I did not actually broadcast myself, and the German Ministry of Information report to this effect, is not true. I was sent to Stalag 8B in Upper Silesia, remaining there until liberated. The treatment was quite good at this camp."

The Portuguese destroyer *DAO* and *HMS Enterprise* were ordered to the last known position of the *Ceramic* to search for survivors. The *DAO* sailed at 0900 on the 9th of December but later reported that she was unable to make headway on account of terrible weather. The ship was obliged to return to Horta having suffered considerable damage. The *Enterprise* did arrive on scene and sent the following message:

"Your 0805A/9. Arrived 090 degrees position of sinkings 250 miles at daylight 11th December. Searched towards position of sinkings at 18 knots zig-zag number 8 until 1255Z/11 when forced to heave to head north. Wind veered from south west force 7 to north force 12 within 15 minutes and in my opinion the resulting heavy confused seas, of typhoon character rendered it virtually impossible for any boat to survive this area. At 1700Z/11 I decided search must be abandoned and to proceed to Clyde when weather permitted. Northerly gale continued until 0600Z/12. After proceeding, a capsized white boat with red bottom color was passed in position 45 degrees 19 minutes north 33 degrees 33 minutes west at 1600Z/12. Nothing else was seen."

The above account by Sapper Munday of the sinking of the *Ceramic* taken after his repatriation in August 1945 and the KTB log entries of the *U-515* are all that are available in official files concerning the incident. The author has not been able to learn of Sapper Munday's endeavors following the war nor of his current status. However, of Kapitänleutnant Werner Henke, skipper of the *U-515*, there is more to tell.

The *U-515* was the most active U-boat of the 10th Flotilla which operated out of Lorient, France. Under Henke's command, the boat sank 28 ships for a total of 177,000 tons until he and his crew were caught by surprise at night on the surface by aircraft from the *USS Guadacanal* (CVE-60) escort carrier group in early April 1944. After suffering unrelenting attacks by air and destroyer units, the U-boat was forced to surface and amidst withering fire at point blank range by destroyer escorts *Flaherty* and *Chatelain*, and aerial rocket and strafing attacks, the boat went to the bottom 175 miles northwest of the Madeira Islands. Forty-four members of the *U-515* were rescued, among them was its skipper, Werner Henke.[22]

In command of the U.S. escort group was Captain Daniel V. Gallery, Jr. who was to later gain fame for his capture of the *U-505*.

When the captured crew was brought on board the *Guadalcanal,* Henke and his officers were put in the ship's brig. Within a few days the ship's chief master at arms had become acquainted with Henke and during one of their conversations the prisoner told him that the British had put out a propaganda broadcast concerning the sinking of the *Ceramic*. They said that they had learned that the ship had been sunk by the *U-515,* and that *Ceramic* survivors had been machine-gunned in their lifeboats. The British added that, "If ever we get anybody from the *U-515* we're going to try them as pirates."

The chief brought this conversation to the attention of Captain Gallery who used a ruse to get Henke and his crew to talk. He called Henke to his cabin and showed him a fake message which ordered him to hand Henke over to the British when the ship refuelled in Gibraltar. To avoid British imprisonment and perhaps a worse end, Henke signed a document agreeing to give information if he would be sent to the United States. Gallery had photo copies made of the signed document and it was passed among the U-boat crew members. Convinced that their skipper had agreed to talk, information began to flow. Henke heard that his crew was cooperating and became recalcitrant.

The U-boat crew was landed at Norfolk, Virginia on 26 April 1944. Henke ended up at Fort Hunt, a special interrogation center located 17 miles south of Washington, D.C. near Mount Vernon. Naval intelligence interrogators continued to threaten him with a transfer to British authorities if he didn't talk. In fact, in June he was informed that he was to be turned over to the Canadians. Henke most likely thought that he would subsequently be given over to the British and perhaps tried as a "pirate."

Shortly after receiving this information, the former U-boat "ace" was shot and killed as he tried to climb over a high wire fence which surrounded the base.[23]

CHAPTER EIGHT

ARCTIC INCIDENT

By February 1945 Allied forces were scoring victory after victory as the noose began to tighten around the Axis countries. That same month saw the recapture of Corregidor by U.S. troops and the landing of our forces on Iwo Jima. In Europe, Allied armored and infantry units reached the Rhine while American and British bombers continued to wreak havoc on German cities. Soviet forces captured Budapest, and Allied leaders met at Yalta to begin post war planning. Within a few months the battle of the Atlantic would be over.[24]

Still, as the war began to near an end, Allied convoys continued to fight their way through Arctic waters and German air and sea attacks to bring vitally needed war materials to Soviet northern ports.

Returning Convoy RA.64, consisting of 34 ships, was scheduled to leave Murmansk and the Kola Inlet on February 17. The

The British Flower Class Corvette H.M.S. BLUEBELL - (Imperial

day prior to its departure Admiral McGrigor, Convoy Commander, ordered all available escort vessels to clear the approaches to the Inlet. *HMS Lark* and *HMS Alnwick Castle* subsequently sent *U-425* to the bottom during a night antisubmarine sweep. However, unknown to the British forces, the Germans had positioned six other U-boats off the entrance to the Inlet.

As the slow moving convoy moved out to sea, the *Lark*'s stern was blown off, probably by *U-968*. However, the badly damaged ship was successfully towed back into the Inlet. Next, the American steamship *Thomas Scott* was hit by torpedo from *U-968* and abandoned prematurely. She was taken under tow by the Soviet destroyer *Zhestkij* and the tug *M-12*. However, she sank before they could reach the harbor.[25]

The worst disaster of the day was the loss of the corvette *Bluebell*. A torpedo from *U-711* exploded in her magazine and she went under in 4 minutes. The Chief Engineer aboard the American ESSO tanker *SS Paul H. Harwood* reported that, "At about 3 p.m. of 17 February, we heard an explosion astern. One of the British destroyers following us was hit, apparently in her magazine. She was only a few cable lengths from us. A steam cloud rose about 500 feet in the air and when it gradually settled down there was nothing left of the vessel . . . After this grim disaster, the convoy assumed close formation and headed north until the time came to turn west."[26] The loss of the *Bluebell* was described by the following official action report dispatched by the skipper of the *HMS Zest*.[27]

From: The Commanding Officer, *HMS Zest*
Date: 26th February 1945
To: Captain (D), Second Destroyer Flotilla

Sinking of the *HMS Bluebell*

The following account of the above is forwarded.

1. About 1522A, 17th February 1945 whilst *Zest* was moving from the port beam, position P on Close Screen, to the port quarter of the convoy, Extended Screen, my attention was called by

the Midshipman of the Watch to the above ship, approximately in position P, by the remark that she appeared to be increasing speed and altering course. I agreed but thought nothing of it until about a half a minute later I saw her blow up.

2. It immediately occurred to me that the ship must have already been in contact with and was actually moving out to attack the U-boat at the moment when the latter sank her. It seemed therefore that there was a good chance of detecting the killer and I ordered the relevant information to be passed to D.17. No trace of this signal can be found in *Zest*'s R/T (Radio Transmission) Log and it seems regrettably certain that it was never passed, probably due to the fact that T.B.S. Watch, whilst leaving harbour and forming up the Convoy, had been kept in the W/T (Wireless Telegraphy) office and was being turned over to Bridge Control at the time when the signal should have gone. A rather similar signal was, however, passed to *Opportune* at 1547.

3. *Zest* reached the scene of the sinking about 1536 when cries were heard from about a dozen men who could just be discerned in the failing light. Although various floats and rafts from the sunk ship were drifting in the vicinity, none were near enough to be of use and I therefore dropped more, though it seems certain that none of the few survivors had the strength even to reach them. If I could have stopped then it might have been possible to rescue the majority of these men but instead I regretfully continued my course to carry out an "Observant" in the hopes of detecting the U-boat.

4. The course to start this from the Datum Point was 300 degrees, the course to which *HMS Bluebell* appeared to have altered immediately prior to being sunk. Whilst on the second leg of the search *Zest* was joined by *Opportune* and on the latter's orders I returned to the sinking to pick up survivors. The whaler was lowered at 1553 at which time there were still three or four voices to be heard, but from scattered sources. I shouted encouragement to them but it was not possible to pick up more than one at a time. Three were actually recovered in an unconscious state, but only one revived, although artificial respiration was continued for nearly 5 hours on the other two.

5. The whaler was hoisted at 1630 and *Opportune* and *Zest* then proceeded to rejoin the screen.
6. I spoke with this survivor, A/P.O. A.E.G. Holmes, Official Number P/JX.217490 next morning, who had been standing on the starboard side by the Engine Room when the ship was struck. He agreed that the ship was increasing speed and said that he had just been sent for by the Captain, possibly to pipe Action Stations (he was Chief Boatswain's Mate). He retained consciousness throughout, was with his Captain afterwards in the water, but did not remember being picked up.
7. As reported in my 180905, the two dead men, Able Seaman *W. H. Butcher,* Official Number not known, and another, now believed to have been Chief Mechanic *Edwards,* Official Number not known, were buried next morning with due honours. The sum of L13.-6d. was found on the former and taken on charge in the Contingent Account. The latter had an unusual cigarette-lighter from which Petty Officer Holmes later deduced his identity.

A. Hicks
Lieutenant Commander R.N.
Commanding Officer

As the convoy RA.64 sailed west it ran into a violent gale which scattered the ships. Convoy escorts were able to shepherd all but four of the ships back together again. On February 20th, the group was intercepted by 25 *Ju-88*s. *Wildcat* fighters from *HMS Nairana* and antiaircraft gunners from aboard the merchant ships put up such a devastating barrage of fire during a 3 1/2-hour battle that the attacking bombers jettisoned their bombs and flew back to their bases.[28]

The convoy was struck again by a hurricane force storm a few days later and the escorts, struggling through deep swells and frigid winds, finally closed the widely scattered group when the convoy again came under attack during the evening hours of the 23rd. Two dozen bombers returned this time and they concentrated their attack on the American Liberty Ship *Henry Bacon,* which because of engine trouble, had fallen behind the main group by some 50 miles. After making a low level run over the ship, the aircraft formed a circle around their prey and attacked in pairs, dropping their torpedoes at point blank range. The U.S. Naval Armed Guard gunners and their merchant mariner counterparts beat off attack after attack until a torpedo hit the ship's magazine and the steamer exploded and began to settle. Sixty-four of the 86 men, women, and children on board (19 were Norwegian passengers) were eventually rescued. The ship's commanding officer, Captain Carini, went down with the ship. The gallant gunners had downed five enemy planes and damaged three others.

Despite heavy seas and stormy weather, Convoy RA.64 finally made it to Gourock on March 1st without further loss. Among those who came ashore was the sole survivor of the *Bluebell*, Chief Boatswain Mate Holmes.[29]

CHAPTER NINE

CONVOY SC.48

''That I verily believe I am the sole survivor of the *W.C. Teagle*.''

Radio Operator N. D. Houston signed the document in an office on 24 Saint Mary Avenue in London on the 24th day of October 1941. A week earlier a sudden explosion rocked his ship and sent him and the entire ship's complement of 45 men into darkened Atlantic waters amidst explosions and burning oil.[30]

The *Teagle* had run smack into a wolf pack of German U-boats and his convoy SC.48 was hit hard, as were the group's escorts, one of which was the American destroyer *USS Kearny*. Kapitänleutnant Joachim Preuss, commandant of *U-568*, fired a single torpedo at the *Kearny*, killing 11 men. Preuss was the first German to cause American military casualties since 1918. Although the United States was not officially at war with Germany, the attack on the *Kearny* and the loss of the destroyer *USS Reuben James* a week later to *U-552* moved both countries to the very edge of war.[31]

Convoy SC.48 the day following the toredoing of the USS KEARNY - (U.S. National Archives)

The last voyage of the *Teagle* began in Philadelphia where the ship had received a thorough overhauling and was degaussed and armed. Originally owned by the Panama Transport Company, *Teagle* was chartered to the U.S. Maritime Commission for United Kingdom service. On September 13, 1941 she departed Philadelphia for Aruba with a British crew of 42 officers and men and a British armed guard of one Navy rating and two Army gunners.

The tanker loaded 96,595 barrels of fuel oil at Aruba and sailed for Halifax, Nova Scotia on the 22nd of September. From Halifax, she joined a convoy gathering at Sydney a few days later. On October 5, *Teagle* joined the 50-ship, 10-column convoy, SC.48, and started out across the Atlantic. The journey was uneventful until the tenth day out, when the U-boats began their attack.

Houston recounted the last hours of the *Teagle* in his statement as follows:[32]

> ". . . the *W.C. Teagle* was in convoy, occupying the third station in the tenth column.
>
> "The wireless receiver had been sealed by the naval authorities and accordingly no continuous wireless watch was being kept. The three radio officers were engaged in assisting the navigating officers on the bridge. (In compliance with British naval regulations in force at the time and instituted by the U.S. Navy after the attack on Pearl Harbor, the wireless receiving set of the *W.C. Teagle* was sealed, since it was of the regenerative type, and any radio messages received by the vessel might be the means of disclosing her position to enemy submarines.)
>
> "At 4:55 a.m. on the 15th I was on the bridge with the chief officer and the men of his watch. The weather was then fine and clear but dark, the wind west northwest, and visibility good. At this time an explosion occurred to the port side of the convoy and shortly afterward I saw the white wake of a submarine proceeding down between the 9th and 10th columns of ships. The white wake disappeared under the stern of the

W.C. Teagle. The presence of the submarine was immediately reported to the naval escort.

"Thereafter, the voyage proceeded without further incident until shortly before 7 o'clock the same evening, when there was considerable activity by the escort at the end of the convoy.

"About 8:40 p.m. on the 16th I was in the chart room with the captain when I heard the sound of an explosion, whereupon I went out on the bridge and saw a glow, as though one of the vessels in the convoy was on fire. The weather at that time was squally with a moderate west northwest wind and freshening with a heavy sea; visibility was good between rain squalls. At 9:20 p.m. I was in my cabin when an explosion occurred in the *W.C. Teagle,* which caused a tremor that was felt throughout the ship. I immediately went to the wireless room and on my way saw that the vessel was illuminated by a fire on the after deck, just forward of the engine room.

"Upon arrival in the wireless room I signalled to the commodore vessel that the *W.C. Teagle* had been torpedoed. Shortly after this I received a call from the bridge by telephone that the tanker appeared to be sinking and that she was being abandoned.

"I left the wireless room and went to the port forward lifeboat. I saw that the fire was being fought by certain members of the crew and they seemed to be getting it under control when the vessel gave a sudden plunge by the stern, precipitating everyone into the water. This occurred about five minutes after the explosion.

"On coming to the surface I saw the bow of the ship standing vertically out of the water and I swam away from her. Shortly afterward I looked to where the ship had been, but she had disappeared.

"I was in the water for about 5 hours until rescued by one of his Majesty's corvettes.

> "I verily believe I am the only survivor of the *W.C. Teagle*."

Captain Erling Vorberg, skipper of the Norwegian tanker *Barfonn*, witnessed the *Teagle* sinking.

> " . . . Soon after 9 p.m. on the 16th I saw the *W.C. Teagle*, which was off my starboard and slightly astern, suddenly aglow and aflame for several minutes; oil from the ship was also blazing on the waters. As the convoy proceeded I saw the ship settling by the stern into the sea.
>
> "From the time the *W.C. Teagle* was struck until several hours later thereafter, many other vessels in the convoy were torpedoed. At about 10 a.m., October 17, my own ship, the *Barfonn*, was hit by a torpedo on the starboard side, and an hour later, as we fell behind the convoy, she was struck again by another torpedo on the starboard side, as a result of which the ship sank. The surviving crew members were picked up by Canadian corvette No. 175 and landed in Iceland."

In addition to the loss of the *Teagle* and the *Barfonn*, SC.48 suffered the loss of the merchant ships *Silvercedar* (British), *Ila* (Norwegian), *Bold Venture* (Panamanian), *Ervikan* (Norwegian), *Rym* (Norwegian), and *Evrons* (Greek). In addition to the damaging of the *U.S.S. Kearny*, two British escort vessels, destroyer *Broadwater* and corvette *Gladiolus*, were sunk by the attacking wolf pack. U-boats scoring successes included *U-553, U-558, U-568, U-432*, and *U-101*.[33]

Silhouetted by a burning merchant ship and forced to come to a stop because of a corvette crossing her bow, the *Kearny* presented a perfect target for *U-568*. Although severely damaged, the American warship was able to get underway about 10 minutes after the torpedo hit and eventually reached Iceland, escorted by the destroyer *Greer*. Blood plasma, badly needed for the *Kearny* casualties, was flown to the scene by a *Catalina* aircraft from Iceland. The plasma was dropped to the ship by parachute.[34]

Houston and other surviving shipmates of convoy SC.48 were among the lucky ones in 1941. During that year some 496 ships totalling 2,421,700 gross tons were lost to Axis forces in North Atlantic waters.[35]

CHAPTER TEN

AIR STRIKE OFF THE GUIANAS

The German U-Boat, *U-512*, a 750-tonner, had a rather short operational career during World War II. She departed Kristiansand, Norway on her maiden war cruise on 15 August 1942. Six weeks later she lay on the bottom of the Atlantic in 42 meters of water off the Guianas. One crewman, Signalman Second Francissik Machon, survived an aerial attack which doomed his boat and shipmates.[36]

Commanded by Kapitänleutnant Wolfgang Schultze, the U-boat recorded its first kill when it sank the 10,000 ton American tanker *Patrick J. Hurley* at 22.59 N/46.12 W on 12 September, 1942. Schultze initially fired two torpedoes at the *Hurley*; both missed. He then decided to attack the steamer with gun fire. He first took up a position dead ahead of the tanker and subsequently veered off to starboard as the tanker began to overhaul his boat. When the tanker was at 300 meters and still somewhat abaft of the U-boat's beam, he opened fire with all of the U-boat's guns. The

10.5 cm fired high explosives: the 3.7 cm incendiary, and the 2 cm bridge A.P. mixed with tracer.

The first shell struck the bridge of the tanker dead on and all subsequent shots were direct hits. After a short interval, fire was returned from the tanker's after gun and some machine gun fire was also observed by crewmen aboard the U-boat. The return fire was ineffective since all shots missed the attacking U-boat.

The tanker began to burn shortly after the attack and was abandoned in about 10 minutes. The U-boat then rounded the stern and fired a few shots into the port side, leaving the vessel on fire and sinking.

After the sinking, Schultze is alleged to have reported home that he had sunk a tanker of 7,500 tons. He received a return message from the Admiral in Command of U-Boats which read roughly as follows: "This ship you sank was not 7,500 but 10,680 tons. It was the *Herlay Patrick* (sic)." This caused great rejoicing among the crew and the victory pennant was prepared showing this tonnage.

A week later Schultze sent the Spanish steamer *Monte Gorbea* to the bottom while patrolling the Antilles. Then, on 24 September, she finished off the American Steamer *Antinous* which had been attacked two days before by *U-515*. However, what promised to be a successful patrol for Schultze and his men ended a week later.

On 2 October a Trinidad-based Douglas *B-18A* of the 99th United States Army Bombing Squadron piloted by Captain Howard Burhanna, Jr., Air Corps, sighted the *U-512* on the surface at 1145Z about 50 miles north of Cayenne. Burhanna was cruising at 5,000 feet in a clear sky with scattered cumulus clouds. The boat was about 8 miles away on a course of 120 degrees.

Burhanna immediately nosed over and changed course to 120 degrees, setting up his attack astern of the unsuspecting U-boat. Four minutes later he passed over the boat at 50 feet doing 210 miles per hour. In quick train, and spaced 40 feet apart, he dropped one 325-, two 650-, and one 325-pound depth charges. At the time of the release of his bombs, the U-boat was still fully surfaced.

The first depth charge entered the water at an estimated 40 feet short of the *U-512*'s stern, and the others appeared to range up along the port side of the submarine very close aboard. Immediately after the attack, air and oil bubbles began rising with gradually increasing intensity. Thirty-seven minutes later, as Burhanna circled the site, a large volume of oil and air bubbles surged to the surface, continuing for about 4 minutes, and spread out into a large circular area. After the attack, a survivor was sighted swimming about in the slick. A life raft and vest were dropped, and the survivor reached both. Burhanna radioed the position of the survivor back to base and left the scene. However, subsequent air patrols were unable to locate the survivor and it wasn't until 10 days later that Signalman Machon was sighted and picked up by the American destroyer *Ellis*.

Signalman Machon was disembarked at Port-of-Spain on 29 October. During his subsequent interrogation he stated that he was 24 years old and of Polish descent. He said he was inducted into the German military service in 1940, and had requested submarine duty at the time.

Shortly before the appearance of the aircraft, Machon had climbed up onto the bridge for a smoke. There was a sudden cry of an enemy aircraft sighting, a crash dive was immediately ordered and the five men on the bridge tumbled below. Machon went forward to his diving station which was at the valves in the galley. Almost immediately, and before the submarine was fully submerged, two direct hits were scored on the boat. They exploded between the 10.5 cm gun and the galley.

The force of the explosion flung Machon diagonally across the boat. He was injured on hitting the opposite bulkhead, wounding himself on the side from the hips down. At the same time a cauldron of soup which was flung into the air landed on his head and caused slight burns.

All illuminations were extinguished except the emergency lights, which burned throughout. Water immediately rushed into the boat and Machon donned his escape lung only to find it useless, as there was no air in the flask.

The boat settled rapidly. Machon remembered that all tanks were blown and the boat's descent was checked momentarily, only to continue downward almost at once. The U-boat sank by the bow which hit the bottom with a sudden jar. The boat came to rest almost level, with little or no list. The depth shown on the torpedo room depth gauge was 42 meters. The water-tight bulkhead door to the bow torpedo compartment had been closed. As the water rose, Machon worked his way forward and beat on it with a fire extinguisher. It was opened to receive him. One emergency light illuminated the room which held 15 men.

Chlorine gas from the batteries of the electric torpedoes engulfed the compartment and the men began to cough. Because of an unfortunate circumstance, there were only four escape lungs in the compartment. A week before the attack, it had been discovered that the escape lungs had been improperly stowed and that the majority had become wet from condensation in the heat. They had consequently been taken aft to the engine room to be dried out.

Three of the men donned their lungs in the hope that they would act as gas masks. Machon donned the remaining escape lung. The air pressure in the compartment began to mount and speech became very difficult. An attempt was made to communicate with other compartments in the boat. One man rang the telephone to the after compartment but collapsed before the call was completed. Machon picked up the dangling instrument and gave the crank another turn. The after compartment replied to his call with the simple statement, "After compartment flooded," and then all communications ceased.

Men were now beginning to collapse rapidly from the combined effect of the chlorine gas and high pressure. Some were bleeding from the mouth and ears. Machon and a boatswain's mate decided to attempt to open the torpedo loading hatch rather than die from the gas. The torpedo hatch was secured with a strongback as well as being dogged shut. Standing at the top of the folding ladder they finally released the strongback and started to open the hatch. Since the loading hatch was at an angle, there was no skirt at the bottom to facilitate escape. As the water rushed in, the two men became wedged in the opening and a struggle resulted. Machon decided to give way to the boatswain's mate, who had no escape lung. Once out, his shipmate appeared to become confused and swam horizontally, only to lose himself between the hull and the superstructure.

Machon followed and after a short struggle succeeded in raising the grating over the torpedo loading hatch. He rose to the surface to find that his escape lung was beginning to burn his mouth. He discarded it, preferring to swim without it. When Machon escaped from the stricken U-boat, the water was at chin level in the compartment.

After what seemed like two hours in the water, an inflated life-jacket was dropped to him from the circling aircraft. This was followed by a rubber raft, outfitted with water, a signal pistol, paddles, and 200 feet of line.

The raft would be Machon's home for the next ten days. His wounds began to fester, and the tropical sun added to his discomfort. The cartridges of his Very pistol were soon used up in a vain attempt to signal passing aircraft and a tanker. In order to escape the heat, he spent a portion of each day in the water. Lashing the empty CO2 flask of the rubber boat and the now useless signal pistol together, he fashioned himself a descending line. He used this means to descend occasionally to a depth where the water was a bit cooler. While there were sharks in the neighborhood, his lot was already so unhappy that he was not much perturbed by their presence. He contented himself with giving one an occasional jab with a paddle as it came to investigate the raft.

At one point he sighted a tanker on a zig-zag course which promised to bring it near. However, the next alteration of course took it farther away. Some time previously one of his two paddles had been carried overboard by a tropical squall. He had arranged it as a signal spar for a piece of rag. As the one paddle would not propel him satisfactorily, he tied the line to himself and swam madly in pursuit of the ship, towing the rubber boat behind him.

Toward the end of his stay on the raft, he was attacked by birds which pecked him on the shoulders so violently as to leave permanent scars. As his provisions had run low he caught and ate two of them, his only food during the ten days he was adrift.

On the 12th of October, Machon was rescued by the *Ellis* at position 07.50 N / 56.05 W. The *Ellis* was on patrol and it was not until October 30 that Machon was landed in Trinidad, B.W.I. His strong constitution, together with the medical care given him on board the *Ellis*, caused a quick and full recovery.

During his interrogation, Machon talked about his commanding officer and his recklessness that might have led to the loss of *U-512* and its crew. Machon stated that Kapitänleutnant Schultze was thoroughly disliked and mistrusted by his crew and considered vain, temperamental, and professionally incompetent. He drank heavily on board and inflicted harsh punishments on his men for minor infractions. Apart from the lowering of morale occasioned by Schultze's strict and unfair discipline, the crew had frequent occasions to grumble over his tactical shortcomings. Believing it his destiny to become a second Prien (famous U-boat ace who sank the British Battleship *HMS Royal Oak* in Scapa Flow in October 1939), Schultze frequently commanded his boat with extreme recklessness. Machon stated that during the boat's trials Schultze was inclined to remain on the surface during simulated aircraft attacks, firing at the planes until he would suddenly dive his boat without warning, leaving the men on deck to swim about until he would surface and pick them up.

Following his preliminary interrogation, Machon was transported to the U.S. where he arrived on November 3, 1942. He eventually was sent to Camp McCain, Mississippi, one of four camps designated for internment of German naval prisoners.

CHAPTER ELEVEN

INFERNO AT SEA

In quiet waters off the South American coast, Kapitänleutnant Adolf Piening, commandant of *U-155* and holder of the Knight's Cross, stalked a low riding tanker flying the British red duster. The year 1942 was proving to be the "happy times" for Hitler's U-boats in the Eastern Atlantic as merchantmen were being sunk in alarming numbers. In fact, in May of 1942, as Piening was about to add another kill to his record, some 90 allied ships totalling 579,650 gross tons were sent to the bottom by German U-boats. American merchant ship losses during that May were the highest for any one month during the war.[37]

As Piening watched his prey he no doubt noticed that the ship looked clean, almost new. The 8,000 ton *San Victorio* was indeed new, she was on her maiden voyage, having departed Aruba a few days before with a full load of aviation fuel. She was sailing independently to her destination, Freetown.[38]

Piening fired two torpedoes, both hit their target; however, the second one blew the ship apart in a volcanic fury. One man survived the catastrophe, a gunner of the Maritime Regiment Royal Artillery, Mr. A. Ryan.[39]

> "We were bound from Curacao to Freetown with a full cargo of benzine and paraffin. We were armed with one-4", two Twin Hotchkiss, two Twin Marlins, one Strip Lewis, four P.A.C. rockets and three Depth Charges. We had a crew of 54, including five Army and three Naval gunners; I regret to say that I am the only survivor of the entire ship's complement. I believe that the Confidential books were all burnt in the ship.We left Curacao about 1400 A.T.S. (Apparent Time at Ship) on May 13th, sailing independently for Freetown. The Captain was aware that submarines were in the vicinity, so we were ordered to double our watches, working 4 hours on and 4 hours off duty. Nothing, however, occurred, the weather was fine with good visibility, the sea was calm with light airs, and we continued zigzagging at a speed of 12 knots until 2000 on May 16th, when we were suddenly struck by a torpedo aft, just forward of the engine-room on the port side. This explosion was not loud and very little water was thrown up.There were four of us at the after gun, we had just changed watch and were on deck waiting for the Sergeant and the Gunlayer to come up. A few seconds later a second torpedo struck the vessel on the starboard side under the bridge; this was a terrific explosion, the ship immediately caught fire and became a blazing inferno. We attempted to go down below to our quarters in order to rescue the other gunners, but this was impossible owing to the flames, so after throwing overboard all the cordite, which was by the gun, the four of us plunged overboard.
>
> "The ship still had weigh on and was burning fiercely down to the water-line. A stream of burning oil was slowly closing round her stern. We realized this, and,

by swimming as fast as we could, we managed to get away from the ship just before she was entirely surrounded by the blazing oil, which had already burnt my back. We had no life-jackets so we had to swim to keep afloat. The water was quite warm, but there was a terrible glare from the sun which was very painful to the eyes. The four of us kept together as much as possible, but after a few hours the others became exhausted and one by one they disappeared below the water. I could see the ship blazing all the time; after about three hours the fire disappeared so I presumed the ship had sunk.

''At about noon on May 17th a submarine chaser, the *U.S.S. Turquoise,* was attacking a submarine in the vicinity. This vessel had sunk one submarine the preceding night (not verified by post war records) and was dropping depth charges on a second. By sheer providence this vessel spotted me and picked me up after I had been in the water 16 1/2 hours. I was quite conscious when picked up, but I could not see, and I felt very weak. After I was safely rescued, however, I completely lost consciousness. I was landed at Trinidad the next day.

''I believe there was a carpenter, who jumped overboard immediately before we did, but I do not know what happened to him afterwards. I also noticed that an aircraft, showing red and green lights, flew over my ship a few minutes after it had been torpedoed, but I do not know whether any report came through.''

(Author's Note: *U-155* was surrendered to Allied Forces in May 1945. The boat, along with over 100 U-boats, was sunk in deep water in the North Atlantic soon after capitulation during British ''Operation Deadlight.''[40])

CHAPTER
TWELVE

SCOTTOCAPO NOSTROMO GIUSEPPE LOCOCO

Ensign T.E. Robertson had been at the controls of his PBY-5A *Catalina* patrol plane (83-P-5) for 10 hours before the sighting. He had lifted off at Natal, Brazil at 0520 hours as part of a five plane anti-blockade runner barrier group. When his bow lookout, S2c Kloss, sighted what he thought was a ship, the lumbering aircraft was at position 3.23 S / 30.38 W.[41]

Second pilot Ensign E.C. Morrison immediately identified the contact as a submarine. Robertson and his co-pilot, Ensign B.S. McCoy, sighted the surfaced sub about 8 miles away on a course of 040 degrees making from 10 to 12 knots. The plane was on a course of 240 degrees, altitude 7,000 feet, and flying at an indicated airspeed of 95 knots. Robertson moved in for the attack.

> "I held my course which carried me about a mile aft of the sub when Morrison told me that the sub was firing on us. Swinging to the port slightly I made a gradual turn to starboard with the sub still to our starboard, losing about 1,000 feet altitude. I decided to make a

Italian submarine ARCHIMEDE (1939-1943) under attack by a VP-83 PBY, April 15, 1943, in the Atlantic Ocean off Natal, Brazil - (U.S. Naval Historical Center)

horizontal bombing run and drop only the two nose fused bombs that were on my starboard wing.

"Morrison was looking at the sub during this time through binoculars. When I started my horizontal run, the sub turned toward me. He was still firing. Our altitude was still about 6,000 feet and I had been on the run for about a minute when Morrison told me over the interphone that the sub was 'going down.'

"Still at 6,000 feet and with the sub a half mile away, I reached for the pickle and put the plane in a steep dive, about 60 degrees, and headed straight for the sub. Tracer bullets were all around the bow during the dive, presumedly from machine guns on the conning tower and possibly from the "pom-pom" type gun on the after end of the conning tower. I released the two depth bombs and the two nose, fused bombs at 2,000 feet and started pulling out of the dive, doing a sharp turn to port. The concussion from the nose fused bombs was sufficiently heavy to make two of our crew members think that the plane had been hit while a third, the tower man, thought that the control cables had given way.

"As I turned to port, I saw exactly where my bombs had landed. The water from the explosions hid the sub completely from view. When everything cleared away, the sub surfaced and started circling to port leaving a streak of brown oil, in addition to bomb residue.

"Much dark grayish smoke was coming directly from and aft of the conning tower. While smoke was visible, the sub seemed out of control. In about 15 minutes the smoke stopped and the sub resumed a direct course. I climbed to 8,000 feet about 6 miles out and continued to circle. I told my radioman to send MOs so the planes in nearby areas could home in on me. While I was circling, the sub's forward 3.5 inch gun was firing irregularly, showing white puffs at the mouth of the gun (ten rounds were actually seen during the 40 minutes before another aircraft arrived). No bursting shells were witnessed at any time.

"One of our squadron mates, 83-P-12, arrived, made a run and dropped his four depth charges which landed very close in. I lost my altitude and combined with 83-P-12 in two of his four strafing runs. I had to pull away twice to avoid a mid-air collision. I made a third run by myself during which the bow of the sub was sticking out of the water at an angle of about 50 degrees. The bow slid backwards and down while I was making the run. By this time the crew of the sub was in the water. I dropped one 7-man raft which landed in the middle of the men. Other rafts were dropped by 83-P-12 before we turned and headed back to base."

What Ensign Robertson didn't know as he and his wingman flew back to their base at Natal was that they had just sunk the Italian submarine *Archimede*. Some 30 to 40 survivors were seen in the water after the attack. Three rafts were dropped but only two were successfully manned; one by 13 survivors and the other by six.

On the twenty-ninth day after the sinking, one raft with a sole survivor washed ashore on the island of Bailique near the western shore of the Amazon River. The survivor was found delirious and very weak by natives who transported him to the nearby Island of Brique. Some days after the prisoner had sufficiently recovered, it was discovered by the natives that he was Italian and a member of the *Archimede*'s crew. The Brazilian naval authorities in Belem were notified of the survivor's presence. The prisoner arrived in Belem on 6 June 1943 aboard a Brazilian gunboat. He was interned incommunicado at the Brazilian naval base, from which he was flown to the United States and arrived at an interrogation center on 27 June 1943.

Under interrogation, the prisoner identified himself as Scottocapo Nostromo (Coxswain, 3cl.) Giuseppe Lococo who had been conscripted in 1938 and had been in the submarine since joining *Archimede* in January of 1939. Lococo described his duties as being a 4-hour daily watch on the conning tower, the operation of the horizontal rudder mechanism in the control room, and loading the forward deck gun. He called his boat ''una carcassa'' (an old hulk). In speaking of the commissioning exercises he expressed the wish that he had never had the honor of raising *Archimede*'s flag nor receiving a billet on her.

Lococo stated that the Italian submarines *Da Vinci, Bagnolini,* and *Archimede* left Bordeaux on 14 February 1943 for a 4 month's cruise. Twenty-five days out, the *Archimede* arrived in her operating zone which was described as a triangle: one leg 500 miles long from Pernambuco to St. Paul Rocks, the second leg 300 miles in a line northwest from St. Paul Rocks, and the base was formed by the line joining the two legs. *Archimede* patrolled the zone without sighting any enemy shipping. At 2400 on 14 April, Lococo clearly saw the lighthouse of San Fernando de Noronha. They continued on a course toward St. Paul Rocks. The following day Lococo and his shipmates met the enemy.

> ''There were some clouds in the sky and the sun was low on the horizon when the first attacking plane appeared. I was in the aft torpedo compartment when I heard the Executive Officer announce over the loudspeaker, 'Plane sighted dead ahead!' Immediately orders were given to man the guns and secure all watertight doors.
>
> ''I ran to my post at the forward deck gun. We were all surprised that the plane made an initial run over our boat without dropping any bombs. We began evasive tactics but made no attempt to submerge. From a point aft of us the plane turned back for a run over us. It dropped two bombs, both missed but one dropped close to the forward starboard side. The concussion from the explosion was terrific, the outer and inner hatches of the forward hatchway were ripped open and away from their hinges and a mountainous wall of water covered the entire boat. In fact, many of us who eventually survived got sick from the quantity of sea water we swallowed during this cascade.

"Because of the damage to the forward hatches we were unable to submerge. The lighting installations had been smashed and one diesel engine had been rendered inoperative. We continued on the surface following an evasive course. The plane in the meantime kept circling at a distance. Suddenly, out of a cloud about 1,000 meters away, a second plane appeared and made a run at low altitude over us. It dropped two bombs which hit the pressure hull aft of the conning tower. One tore through the aft hatchway, and a sheet of flame burst from the oil deposit at the bottom of the hatchway. The four primed torpedoes in the aft tubes also exploded.

"The explosions ripped a tremendous hole in the pressure hull, and the aft torpedo compartment hung like a broken arm from the rest of the boat. Our boat suddenly plunged stern first beneath the surface with our bow high in the air. I was peppered by many metal fragments in the second bomb attack. At the point of a gun, our engineering officer held many of the crew below. Twenty-five of us including the commanding officer succeeded in getting into the water free of our sinking boat. Of these, however, six were drowned either because of wounds or burns from flaming oil.The machine gun on the port side of the aft conning tower had been rendered useless during the first bombing attack, but the starboard machine gun manned by Scottocapo Motorista Votero continued to fire until the water reached his neck. He was badly wounded in one leg and died shortly after he was pulled aboard a raft.

"Three rubber rafts were dropped by the planes but only two were recovered. I swam about 100 meters to recover them. I inflated them, tied one in tow and rowed to the other survivors. One raft was manned by thirteen including the Captain, Guido Saccardo, the Executive Officer, two junior ratings and myself. In the other there were six ratings. The two rafts, tied together, drifted as the occupants were too weak to row. We all felt that we were drifting toward the Antilles.

"On the day after the sinking as well as on the following day planes were seen circling around at a distance. Some of us stood up and blew little whistles furnished in the rafts. We had practically no clothing for signalling. On the fifth day adrift, a steamer was sighted on the horizon but again we had no success in signalling its attention. Again, on the seventh day, a steamer which one of the men believed to be Argentinian, passed about 1,200 meters away at approximately 10 knots.

"Captain Saccardo transferred to the raft with the six men, borrowed two oars from our raft and set off in the direction of the ship. He promised to return for the rest of us if he were successful. Nothing was seen or heard of the commander and his companions after that. I doubted that he ever succeeded in reaching the ship.

"We drifted on, one by one the men in our raft died either from wounds, burns, hunger, thirst or from drinking too much sea water. Finally, there was just a shipmate, Zuliani, and myself left after twenty days at sea. He succumbed a week later. I was alone.

"I had a narrow escape on the twenty-eighth day adrift, the raft overturned throwing me into the water but the next wave righted the raft and threw me back into the raft. This incident reminded me that Zuliani, before dying, had assured me that I would be the sole survivor.

"On the twenty-ninth day after the sinking my raft washed ashore and I was found by two fishermen."

Lococo was subsequently handed over to U.S. authorities. After interrogation he was interned in a POW camp in Mississippi and later repatriated to Italy at the end of the war. A review of a copy of his service record indicates that he received the Italian "War Cross for Military Valor" for submarine battle action in September 1941.

CHAPTER
THIRTEEN

SCORE ONE FOR THE "LITTLE BOYS"

Kapitänleutnant Klaus Bargsten, Commandant of *U-521*, was resting in the bunk of his small cabin on June 2, 1943, reading a translation of the Lynds' *Middletown*. The boat was submerged, moving slowly towards the Capes of Delaware. He had left Lorient, France in company with *U-66* at the end of April 1943 to operate off the American coast. Although the U-boat "happy days" of 1942 in U.S. coastal waters had passed, there were still numerous targets of prey for Dönitz's grey wolves in the Western Atlantic.[42]

Bargsten was an "ace," having been awarded the Knight's Cross for sinking some 30,000 tons of shipping during a previous 79-day patrol.[43] Above him, a Guantanamo-bound convoy approached. The churning blades of convoy propellers went unheeded by his sound operators and the Type IXC boat continued on course.

Suddenly, the convoy was overhead and, as a sound operator rushed into Bargsten's cabin to report the contact, the U-boat was

Kapitanleutnant Klaus Bargsten, Commandant U-521 - (U.S. National Archives)

pounded with close-in depth charges. Instruments were shattered, the lights went off, the motors stopped, rudder and diving planes were rendered useless, and water entered the control room through the depth gauge and tank pressure gauge connections.

Bargsten at once gave the order to dive, although he didn't know the extent of the damage received. After a few seconds, the Engineer Officer reported that the boat was at 150 meters. Bargsten told him that was "nonsense," but the engineer insisted and called off further readings from the control room depth gauge: "160 meters; 170 meters." Later on, Bargsten realized that the U-boat could not have descended to the depths called off by the Engineer Officer without becoming heavy by the bow or by the stern, whereas she kept an even keel throughout. The order was given to blow all tanks, and the boat rose rapidly to the surface. Upon breaking surface, Bargsten went to the bridge to make a topside estimate of the situation.

The American patrol craft (*PC-565*), which had been escorting Convoy NG.355 and had made contact and dropped a standard five charge pattern of depth charges on *U-521*, was about 400 yards from the U-boat when it appeared on the surface. The patrol craft fired about 55 rounds with her 20 mm. gun, scoring several hits on the conning tower. Her gun jammed as she was turning to ram the target. Another escort vessel, *PG-89*, named *USS Brisk*, fired a shell from her No. 1 gun and missed the U-boat by about 50 yards. She ceased firing then, as *PC-565* was in the line of fire.[44]

When Bargsten observed the maneuvers of *PC-565* and saw the patrol craft bearing down on him, he realized the U-boat's position to be hopeless and gave the order to flood and abandon ship. It was not until he saw his Engineer Officer coming up through the conning tower that he realized that the officer had become panicky, since the Engineer's station was in the control room. *U-521* then suddenly sank, leaving Bargsten swimming in the water. His last view of the boat was of water pouring down the conning tower hatch as she went under.

When the U-boat disappeared, *PC-565* altered course to the right to pass ahead of the swirl. At 1243Q she dropped one depth charge set at 100 feet about 100 yards ahead of the position of the sinking. She then moved in to pick up the survivor and several large air slugs were observed. The patrol craft continued to search the area and at 1325Q several oil slicks were sighted. One slick was dark with globules of brown oil, but it was not iridescent. The second slick was larger. The oil lay in heavy patches on the surface and was indeed iridescent. Patches of vegetable fibre and splinters of freshly broken wood were observed. At 1338Q, *PC-565* picked up a large piece of human flesh. The search was abandoned at 1430Q.

At 0045 on 3 June, *USS Chickadee* conducted a box search in the vicinity of the sinking. Results were negative. At daylight, an oil slick was seen, originating at the approximate position of the sinking and extending approximately 060 degrees for 19.7 miles. Its width varied from 25 yards to 300 yards. Samples of the oil were taken and after analysis proved to be lubricating oil.

Operating on the theory that the U-boat was not sunk but was proceeding submerged and bleeding oil, *Chickadee* conducted a box search in the vicinity of the origin of the slick. The results were again negative. It was observed that the current was flowing in the direction of the wind, 060 degrees True. The conclusion was reached that the combined effect of wind and current caused the great length of the oil slick and that, in fact, the U-boat had been sunk.

During his subsequent interrogation, Bargsten told many anecdotes about events and personalities in the German Navy.

While he was serving as a midshipman on Hitler's yacht, *Grille*, Bargsten had occasion to see many of the leading members of the Nazi party. Once, he said, when a group of Olympians was aboard, an orchestra was playing for their entertainment, but the ship's ventilators were making so much noise that the music could scarcely be heard. Goebbels complained to the captain in his usual high handed manner, ordering him to do something about it. The captain, while engaging Goebbels in conversation, managed to back him into position in front of one of the ventilators. When he gave the order for the ventilators to be shut off, the shutter gave Goebbels a resounding whack on the back side.

Bargsten also spoke somewhat heretically about the alcoholic habits of the Nazi hierarchy. Hitler, he said, objected strenuously to drinking and often gave his staff violent temperance lectures. Shortly after having been subjected to one such harangue on board *Grille*, the staff gathered in the saloon to sooth their frayed nerves with a bottle of champagne. Suddenly, Hitler appeared in the doorway and the bottle, which had just been opened, was discretely hidden beneath the table. Hitler strode into the room, kicked the bottle, spilling its contents, turned on his heel, and walked out without uttering a word.

Several unusual accidents to U-boats were described by Bargsten. He related the well-known story of how *U-43* commanded by Kapitänleutnant Lüth sank at the pier in Lorient in January 1941 because the men on watch failed to notice an open vent. At that time Oberleutnant Bernbeck of the 1934 Naval Term was Executive Officer and Oberleutnant Erwin Witte of the 1935 Naval Term was the Second Watch Officer. They were both held responsible for the accident by a board of inquiry in Berlin and were required to pay for the repairs to the boat. These repairs lasted 5 months and included the installation of new electric motors. Neither officer was promoted following this incident.

Regarding signals, Bargsten spoke of a message that Dönitz sent to Prien (the Scapa Flow "Ace") on the occasion of the birth of Prien's daughter. The message read: "Ein U-boot ohne Sehrohr ist heute angekommen" (A submarine without periscope arrived today).

Bargsten stated that listening to British broadcasts, while forbidden in Germany, was quite common. He said that severe penalties were dealt out, not for listening, but for spreading news. When Bargsten's friend, Oberleutnant Hans Ey, Captain of *U-433*, was captured in November 1941, the news of his rescue was later broadcast on a British program. On the day of the broadcast, Ey's wife received three anonymous telephone calls and on the following day, eight anonymous letters congratulating her on the good news.

Bargsten told of how officer candidates at U-boat school were required to pump out the heads of a U-boat at a depth of about 20 meters. After successfully performing this act, they were presented with a "W.C. Schein" (W.C. Certificate) which described in a facetious way their great acts of heroism.

Bargsten stated that in his opinion the greatest tactical aid in escape maneuvers was the S.B.T. (Submarine Bubble Target—used to deceive allied attacking antisubmarine forces). He attributed his own escape from *U-563* from a destroyer attack to this device and said many other U-boats had been saved by its employment.

With regard to the loss of his boat, Bargsten was particularly upset by the fact that he had been defeated by a 173-foot patrol craft commanded by an officer with only 2 years of naval service. Lieutenant Walter T. Flynn USNR was inexperienced and was often chided for his overeagerness. But when his moment came, he and his crew met the challenge and scored a momentous victory.

Following his interrogation, Kapitänleutnant Bargsten was transferred to the Prisoner of War Facility at Camp Blanding, Florida. He was repatriated back to Germany at the end of the war.

HMS NEPTUNE sole surivivor seaman John Norman Walton

HMS NEPTUNE (British Cruiser, 1933) - (U.S. Naval Historical Center)

CHAPTER FOURTEEN

THE MINEFIELD

During 1941 British and Axis forces struggled for control of the Mediterranean Sea. General Rommel and his Afrika Korps were moving swiftly westward across North Africa towards the Suez Canal. His success depended on an open supply line from southern Europe. British naval forces and aircraft flying from airfields on the island of Malta fought fiercely to halt southbound Axis convoys. Royal Navy surface combatants enjoyed a series of successful encounters during the year. However, in December the "Malta Striking Force," as it was called, ceased to exist.[45]

At 1830 on 18 December the Malta Striking Force, commanded by Captain R. C. O'Conor, who was aboard the cruiser *HMS Neptune,* passed through the Malta breakwater, followed a swept channel and then turned to a course of 196 degrees to intercept an enemy convoy consisting of a cruiser, three destroyers, and three merchant ships. O'Conor's group included the cruisers *Neptune, Aurora* (Captain Agnew), and *Penelope* (Captain Nichol), and destroyers *Lance, Lively* (Lcdr. Hussey), *Kandahar* (Cdr. Robson), and *Havock* (Lcdr. Watkins). As the ships sped forward at 30 knots into the night darkness, they were met by a stiffening southwest wind and intermittent rain squalls.

At about midnight the Force had reached a position 20 miles from Tripoli Harbor. O'Conor ordered his following line of ships to decrease their speed down to 24 knots. As he was about to turn and follow a course parallel to the coastline, disaster struck quickly. The British force had steamed unknowingly into a field of special German contact mines which had been laid earlier by Italian cruisers. At 0010 the *Neptune* suffered an explosion off her starboard bow. As she came to all stop and then slow astern she hit another mine which damaged her propulsion and steerage gear. The *Aurora,* following behind, immediately pulled out of line only to be struck by a mine to her port, abreast of her "B" turret. She immediately listed to port and settled by the bow. Counterflooding, reduced speed, and a course change to 020 degrees saved the cruiser from going down.

Captain Nichol in the *Penelope* thought that the *Neptune* and *Aurora* had been hit by torpedoes and turned to starboard to avoid a similar fate. She too was struck abreast of the bridge. However, only minor damage was inflicted since she was streaming paravanes and the mine detonated in these.[46]

The next ship, *Kandahar,* closed the *Neptune* and when abreast of her a third mine exploded under the cruiser's port quarter. The *Neptune* was now critically damaged and had lost all steam and power. Captain Agnew, now as senior officer, sized up the situation and decided that the *Aurora* would be vulnerable to enemy air attacks if she remained in the area after daylight. He set course for Malta with destroyers *Havock* and *Lance* as escorts and arrived safely back at Malta at 1230 on the 19th of December. The *Aurora* subsequently went on to Gibraltar for repairs where she remained out of action for 13 weeks.

Penelope and *Lively* closed *Neptune* and prepared to take her in tow as soon as she cleared the minefield. However, another explosion, this time under the stern of *Kandahar,* forced the *Penelope* and *Lively* to back off. Both *Neptune* and *Kandahar* signalled the two ships to "Keep away!" Another explosion and flash were seen at 0200 when the *Neptune* hit yet another mine. The ship quickly heeled to port and capsized. Unbeknownst to the other ships, one man, Seaman John Norman Walton, survived the *Neptune* ordeal. Adrift on a raft for six days, "Gordie" Walton was later rescued by an Italian destroyer and eventually transported to an Italian Prisoner-of-War camp. He was repatriated to the United Kingdom at the end of the war with Germany.

Captain Nichol aboard the *Penelope* realized there was nothing more he could do to help the *Kandahar*. He signalled, "I clearly cannot help. God be with you."

Penelope and *Lively* set course for Malta and requested that Rear-Admiral Malta send a submarine or Sunderland flying boat to rescue the companies of the mined ships.

The stern of the *Kandahar* had been completely blown off and her stern abaft her funnel was under water. The only available ship at Malta which could sail to the aid of her sister ship was the *Jaguar*. *Jaguar* departed Malta on December 19 at 1625 hours and with the help of *ASV Wellington*, the ship found the *Kandahar* and successfully rescued eight officers and 160 ratings. She later torpedoed the stricken vessel to prevent her from falling into enemy hands.

And so the Malta Striking Force was lost. It was never reconstituted as before. The few remaining ships attached to the unit served as convoy escorts. However, with the arrival of the *Luftwaffe's Fliegerkorps II* and the massive air assaults soon to devastate Malta, it is questionable whether the naval force could have ultimately survived.

Seaman Walton kept a diary of his experiences during the war and what follows is his remembrance of the *Neptune's* final hours, his survival, capture and repatriation. This is the first time that Seaman Walton has provided his personal account for publication.

> "We steam out of Grand Harbour, Malta, aboard *HMS Neptune*, Captain Rory O'Conor commanding, at 1830 hours on 18th December 1943 as a member of K Force."

"At 2350 hours, the Captain announces that we will probably meet up with an enemy convoy between 0300 and 0400 hours. All hands are at action stations. As Submarine Detector my station is in the ASDIC cabin. Having been closed up at action stations since 2000 hours, we finally get news as to where we're going and why. We departed from Malta on a crash order to prepare for sea and sailed in record time. We're now cruising at 30 to 32 knots.

"At 0010 hours on the 19th there is an explosion off the starboard bow. Our starboard paravane has been blown away. The Captain orders all stop then slow astern, we hit another mine and our screws and rudder are severely damaged, leaving us without steerage and adrift.

"A little after midnight we hit another mine on the port side abaft the funnel. We now are listing heavily to port and are down by the stern. Our Commander (Berry) asks for a few ratings to go forward and prepare the ship for towing. I volunteer along with six others. Suddenly, *HMS Kandahar* hits a mine and as *HMS Lively* swings around our stern to come up along our starboard side she is ordered away by Captain O'Conor.

"Just as I finished putting a chain stopper on the tow rope and walked forward to assist the "Captain Petty Officer" of the fo'c'sle on the cable we hit our fourth mine. The explosion lifted us off the deck and as I dropped back onto the deck I caught hold of a guard rail. Looking around I saw the "Captain Petty Officer" underneath the anchor cable. Making my way to him I found him dead, crushed by the explosion. I heard the captain sing out, "Abandon Ship!" It was about 0200 hours.

"By this time most of the crew had gone over the side. Acting Leading Seaman Price, Able Bodied Seaman Quinn (New Zealand), Able Bodied Seaman Middleton and myself left on the fo'c'sle. We climbed down onto the anchor and as they jumped overboard, looked for something to hang onto in the water. I saw a carley raft, jumped in and swam for it. Reaching it easily, I thought of little Jock Middleton with no life belt. I found a rope which was attached to the raft and got it to Jock who was hanging onto Quinney and Pricey a short way from the raft. We hauled him back to the raft with us which was now crowded. We got Jock onto it anyway and the rest of us hung on to the side. There were about 30 of us or more.

"We cheered as the ship slipped beneath the sea. The last to disappear was the Union Jack waving gently on the Bow Jack staff. We soon picked up the captain who had been hanging onto what looked like an anchor bouy. A cork raft came into sight and we secured it to our raft. The captain, our antisubmarine officer, a commissioned gunner and one other officer, perhaps the paymaster lieutenant, manned the cork raft. As we looked out into the night air we could see the flashing lights of the other K Force ships.

"A number of men died around us that night. Many from wounds suffered during the mine explosions, others to exposure since the water was very cold and drenched in oil. A few just gave up. By daylight, 16 remained alive. The antisubmarine officer and the commissioned gunner decided to swim to the *Kandahar* which we could see at times over the rough seas. I learned later that they didn't make it. As aircraft flew over us during the forenoon, three more ratings died."

"We picked up an oar and broke it trying to make land. We gauged the position of the sun, attempting to fix the time of day while we continued to drift, making no headway. By the fourth day there was only four of us left including the captain who passed away that night. The only words he spoke the entire time we were adrift was on the first night when he said that we were only four miles off Tripoli when our ship went down.

''On the afternoon of the 24th, Christmas Eve, there were two of us left, Pricey and myself. He was almost gone. I sighted an airplane and tried signalling it, but it disappeared leaving us again alone on the open sea. An hour or so later an Italian destroyer with the letters C.P. marked on its side came alongside the raft. They threw a heaving line which I caught and secured around Price, though I knew it was too late for him. He was dead. They threw another which I tried to secure to the raft, then as I tried to climb onto the propeller guard of the ship I passed out.

''When I came to on the ship I was surrounded by men speaking a language I couldn't understand. I drifted in and out of consciousness until I finally woke up in a hospital bed in Tripoli.''

''Following a short period of recovery, I was taken to Bari, Italy and interned in Campo 75 which was a distribution point for allied prisoners-of-war. I eventually was taken to Campo 65 located near Granvinia and left there to sit out the war.

''After I had been there awhile we got our first Red Cross parcels. What a Godsend! To pass the time we went about building a basketball pitch. Not many of us knew the game, it was more of an army game. However, we soon mastered it and started a league. In the five finals we had in the camp, we, the ''Marlots,'' won it once and were runners up four times. We struggled on, more or less the same way all the time—we were prisoners—our thoughts were always the same, food and freedom.

''On the 6th of March 1943, about 20 of us Marlots left Campo 65 and returned to Bari. There, we learned that we were being repatriated in exchange for Italian soldiers. Italy was on the verge of packing it in then.

''We sailed on board the hospital ship *Grandisca* for Mersin, Turkey on 14th March where the exchange was to take place. We arrived on the 19th and I was freed

> and taken aboard the British ship *HMS Talma* on the 21st. After fighting off a bout of malaria at our first port to call, Alexandria, we started on our long trek home. We transited the Suez Canal, sailed down the Red Sea of Durban, South Africa, then on to Cape Town. We next crossed the South Africa, then on to Cape Town. We next crossed the South Atlantic stopping at Rio de Janeiro, then onto ports along the U.S. Atlantic coast and Canada, then finally on to England and home. I enjoyed a most wonderful three weeks leave with my Mum and Dad, my four younger brothers and four younger sisters. I had been away nearly four years.[47]''

Seaman Walton, however, continued to serve his country following his return to England. After a short period of rest and recuperation he was ordered aboard *HMS Challenger* (a surveying vessel) stationed in the Pacific.

While aboard the *Challenger,* Walton became good friends with Edward ''Gordie'' Gallagher who was also from Newcastle, England. British history records that when King George travelled north to put down the Scottish Rebellion, he stopped at Newcastle where he was supplied with food and fodder. Before he departed the city numerous Newcastle men had joined his army and fought bravely in the subsequent struggle. From then on the men of Newcastle became known as ''Gordies'' men, meaning King George's men. Thus, all ''Gordie's'' serving aboard His Majesty's ships during the war were bonded by this heritage.

''Gordie'' Gallagher recalled that one day Walton took him into his mess and showed him letters from hundreds of people asking if it was possible that their sons, husbands, etc. had a chance to survive. All of the letter envelopes were addressed to

Petty Officer Walton
Only Known Survivor *HMS Neptune* [48]

CHAPTER FIFTEEN

DOWN OFF GREECE!

Leading Stoker John Capes, a submariner, served in Malta before the war broke out where he got involved in a situation that seemed like it would never end. Years later, in September 1941, he made his way back to the island from Alexandria to try and resolve the matter which involved a horse-drawn cab and a hired car. Months of haggling proved fruitless and in November he was directed to return to Alexandria. On 24 November he found passage on board the British submarine *HMS Perseus* which was commanded by Lieutenant Commander E.C.F. Nicolay. Fate had played its hand, for John Capes was soon to experience one of the more extraordinary survival escapes of the war.

The *Perseus* cast off its lines on the 26th and sailed for the Aegean Sea where it was to patrol east of Greece before proceeding to Alexandria. Several days into the voyage, the sub fired torpedoes at two vessels. Capes got the impression from comments made by other crewmen that both targets were destroyed.[49]

British submarine HMS PERSEUS, June 25, 1930 - (National Maritime Museum)

At 2200 hours on 6 December, there was a terrific explosion, which Capes thought was due to the submarine striking a mine. All starboard ballast was lost and the submarine assumed an angle of 90 degrees. She sank rapidly and touched bottom bow first. Finally, she settled full length on the sea bed, while retaining a sizeable starboard angle. At the time of the explosion, Capes was standing by the steering wheel in the after end where he received a considerable blow to his posterior by some flying object. Every pipeline and valve in the after end and rear compartments was broken. All lighting failed within 15 minutes of the explosion.

Capes found that of the crew of 55, only five besides himself showed life after the submarine had finally settled. There were no officers, petty officers, or sailors alive, only five other stokers, all from the afterend and rear compartments.

Capes felt certain that all forward personnel must have been instantly killed by the explosion and subsequent flooding.

Eventually, two lamps of the secondary lighting system were found and switched on and the D.S.E.A. (Davis Submarine Escape Apparatus) was retrieved from lockers and donned. (The D.S.E.A. consisted of a small air cylinder supplying a mouthpiece, a nose clip, and a buoyancy aid. The whole affair was worn with a harness over the torso. There was also an apron, which was held out at right angles by the wearer during the ascent to control the speed, and a battery-operated light used for signalling on the surface.)

The submarine was next flooded by means of the underwater gun, which raised the water rapidly to about 3 1/2 to 4 feet. The hatch trunking was then pulled down.

A pipe was disconnected from the high pressure air line and the valve cracked slightly open to allow air to enter the afterend compartment. It was felt that the compartment would soon be completely flooded without chance of escape, since the water was rising rapidly owing to punctures of the exterior hull. The D.S.E.A. hatch clips were taken off and the trunking was then attached to the deck. All this was done with extreme difficulty, since the starboard ship's side was now being used as a deck.

And, to make matters worse, a drum of oil and one of enamel had burst and greased the water, making it hard to keep the D.S.E.A. nose clips on.

At this time only one other stoker besides Capes was alive as the submarine re-settled itself on the bottom, taking on a still steeper starboard angle. Pressure on the Z tank first showed 60 pounds; however, after the submarine re-settled, the gauge was on full stop, showing 70 pounds or more. Capes attempted to leave with the D.S.E.A. using the light but, owing to the blast of air coming through the D.S.E.A. canvas trunking, he was forced to return to the compartment. Capes re-fitted his nose piece and re-entered. As the outside hatch jumping wire was not visible, he proceeded slowly on his own to the surface. Using the D.S.E.A. apron, he controlled the speed of his ascent. As he drew nearer to the surface, he saw a mine and judged it to be at a depth of ten to fifteen feet.

On surfacing, Capes used his light to send S.O.S. signals towards land, but there was no answer, nor were there any signs of other survivors in the sea around him. He judged the time taken to escape the boat and reach the surface from the time of explosion to be about 1 1/2 hours.

Capes estimated that the nearest shore was 5 or 6 miles away. He immediately began to swim and made landfall some 6 hours later. He was extremely weak and fearful of being seen by a sentry whom he had sighted on a hill one-half mile away as he was on the last leg of his swim. However, he safely reached a small cave. At about 1000 hours, two villagers entered the cave and were quite surprised to find him there.

What began now for Capes was a 16-month venture by the Greek patriots to hide him from the Italian Carabinieri. He was moved from house to house, sometimes just one step ahead of the enemy.

Finally, on June 2, 1943, he was embarked on a boat to Kioste and safety.

John H. Capes, sole survivor of the *HMS Perseus,* received the British Empire Medal (Military) on December 1, 1943. His commendation, written by Captain Ruck Keene, commanding 1st SM Flotilla at Alexandria, read:

> "This rating was in the after end of *HMS Perseus* when she was sunk apparently by a mine off Cephalonia on 6th December 1941. By great courage, perseverance and calm judgment he effected an escape by the D.S.E.A., under what must have been most trying conditions, which is as successful an attempt as has ever been made, as he must have been considerably shaken; so great had been the force of the explosion of the mine that all but five of the crew were apparently killed almost instantaneously. The submarine sank bow down at an almost perpendicular angle, and she was laying on the bottom heeled to starboard. After making good his escape from the submarine he swam ashore and was looked after by the Greeks. Largely helped by his own skill, tenacity and perseverance he succeeded in escaping."

Capes eventually returned to naval service and remained on duty for several years after the end of the war.

CHAPTER SIXTEEN

CLIFFORD W. KUYKENDALL, GM2/c, USN

"To those whose contribution meant the loss of sons, brothers or husbands in this war, I pay my most humble respect and extend my deepest sympathy. As to the 374 officers and 3131 men of the Submarine Force who gave their lives in the winning of this war, I can assure you that they went down fighting and that their brothers who survived them took a grim toll of our savage enemy to avenge their deaths.

MAY GOD REST THEIR SOULS"
From speech given in Cleveland, Navy Day 1945,
by Vice Admiral C.A. Lockwood, Jr.,
Commander Submarine Force, U.S. Pacific Fleet,
January 1943-January 1946.[50]

Fifty-two U.S. Navy submarines made final patrols during World War II. They represented approximately 18 percent of all

USS TULLIBEE (SS 204) - (U.S. National Archives)

submarines which saw combat duty. The U.S. Silent Service accounted for the destruction of 201 naval vessels and 1,113 merchantmen flying Axis colors during the war.

In the case of losses due to enemy action, three officers and five men from the *Flier* and all but four men from *Sealion* were saved. The remaining submarines were lost with all hands, although some personnel from *Grenadier, Perch, Scuplin, Tang,* two men from *SS-44,* and one from *Tullibee* were repatriated at the end of hostilities, having been held as prisoners of war by the enemy.[51]

The sole survivor of the *Tullibee* was Clifford W. Kuykendall, GM2/c, 356-73-89. His account of survival is similar to that of other submariners who were taken prisoner by the Japanese.[52]

> "We arrived on station March 25th, 1944, Northwest of Palau Island. During the daytime we stayed on the surface making three practice dives per day. At night we cut the speed down to 1/3. On March the 26th at about 0800 we made radar contact at 24,000 yards. We began moving in on the target and as we drew closer we found out that it was a large troop and cargo ship.
>
> "Astern of the large transport were two medium sized freighters. The convoy was escorted by two Jap escort vessels and one large destroyer. The small escort vessels were out in front and the destroyer was astern of the convoy bringing up the rear. We were making several runs on the convoy getting the range, angle on the bow, speed and zigzag course the ships were steering.
>
> "We started to make a torpedo run but the Captain wanted to be able to see the target before firing. After making two torpedo runs (radar approaches) on the target the Japanese escort vessels began dropping depth charges, using their search lights and signalling to the other ships in the convoy with their blinker lights.
>
> "They dropped between 15 and 20 charges, then stopped and didn't drop any more. We had selected

the large transport as our target. We made three torpedo runs but were not able to see the target and did not fire. On the 4th torpedo run we went in about 3,000 yards, still unable to see the target, but fired two torpedoes anyway from the bow. In less than two minutes after firing, a terrific concussion shook the boat. I was pretty positive that the explosion was the result of a circular run by one of our own torpedoes.

"Positioned on the bridge I was immediately knocked unconscious by the concussion and when I came to I was struggling in the water. I was practically drowned but was able to inflate the life belt which I was wearing. I could hear men yelling around me in the water and I yelled back but could never tell what they were saying or where they were.

"There was a very thick oil slick covering the water around me. Ten minutes after I regained consciousness I saw the *Tullibee* about 75 yards distance from me, it was going down by the stern and the after part of the conning tower was sinking below the waves. A large dark low flying rain cloud came between the sub and myself and I didn't see the sub again or see it go down. All of this happened between 0300 and 0315.

"At daybreak I looked around for signs of other men besides myself or floating debris, but I was the only floating thing in the water. Nothing else could be seen but a thin oil slick on the water.

"At 1000 I saw an escort vessel at a range of about 6,000 yards which was coming directly toward me from due west. At about 3,000 yards the vessel made a sharp port turn. When due south of me he sighted me and began circling. All port machine guns opened fire, the vessel made a complete 360° circuit around me firing all the time. As a result I suffered five separate flesh wounds.

"After making a complete circuit the vessel came alongside me and picked me up. First thing after being pulled on deck an English speaking officer struck me alongside the head with a large club and knocked me unconscious. After I came to this Officer along with another English speaking officer began questioning me. The information that they wanted to know was the name of the submarine, the captain's name, where we were operating from, names of the crew, length, dimensions, type of guns and all details covering the submarine. This continued all day but I stuck to international law only giving them my name, rate, service number and service.

''I was treated terribly by the two officers who did all the beating. They beat me with clubs, raw hide thongs, rifle stocks, and hit me alongside the head with a pistol barrel. They said that they were going to behead me with a saber and made several swings over my head with it before changing their mind and securing the weapon.

''At about 1630 we arrived in port and anchored in a harbor between two islands. I was questioned again on deck and beaten some more then put into a launch, blindfolded, and taken ashore. After arriving ashore I was taken somewhere by car and put into a storeroom for the night. Two sentries were placed outside the door.

''The next morning I was questioned by three officers through an interpreter. I responded as before. The interpreter said that if I didn't tell them all they wanted to know they would kill me. On March 29th, I was transferred from the storeroom to a brig which I found out later was closer to the beach.

''Early in the morning of the 30th I heard antiaircraft fire, then planes. At first I didn't realize what was happening but then I knew it was a raid. Bombs began falling and fighters began strafing the area around me. Explosions destroyed my cell window and I could now clearly see our own planes dive bombing and strafing the island and the other island across the bay. I never did see a Jap plane in the air.

''The strafing set on fire ammunition dumps some 50 yards from the brig and ammunition began exploding, destroying the brig I was in and leaving me under the debris. I was removed by two Japs and taken to a tunnel located underground. After dark, I was removed and taken into the hills and tied to a tree for about 55 hours. I was not given water or food during this time. I was later taken to a village that was located along the beach and kept in a dugout until April 5th.

''I was next taken to a seaplane in the bay and flown to some island in the Marianas group. I stayed there for two days and was questioned once again by an interpreter. They wanted to know the same information I had been previously asked and once again I stuck to International Law. I was finally flown to Yokohama on April 7th.

''After my arrival, I was taken by bus and train to Ofuna Naval Interrogation Camp where the guards beat the prisoners daily. I stayed in this camp until September 30, 1944. During this time, I was interrogated by Japanese Naval officers. They questioned me about all details of submarine operations and war patrols, bases of operation and other naval vessels. I was also asked about the rules and regulations of the United States Navy.

''The interrogation completed, I was transferred to a labor camp located in the mountains about 100 miles north of Tokyo. I worked in the copper mines from October 3rd, 1944 to August 15, 1945. The mine was underground and the labor was very, very hard. The food was very bad and the living conditions filthy. Our barracks were poorly constructed. They were unheated in the winter and full of lice, fleas and rats. Prisoners working the mine were beaten by Jap work foremen if they didn't like the way prisoners were working. This happened daily. The Japanese stopped all work details on August 15th and we left camp on September 4th for Yokohama.

"Throughout this time I remembered the words of the Jap officer aboard the destroyer that picked me up. He said, 'Why don't you admit you are off the submarine that attacked the convoy and sunk the ship the night before?' From this I would say that one of our torpedoes did indeed find its mark that night."

CHAPTER
SEVENTEEN

BATTLE OFF NARVIK

As the last Royal Air Force *Hurricane* fighter touched down on the carrier *HMS Glorious* in the early morning hours of 7 June 1940, the deck crew scurried about tying down the land-based aircraft in preparation for their journey home.

The British campaign against the German outpost at Narvik, Norway had been completed and with Germany marching successfully through the low countries and France, the Narvik force was ordered home. *Hurricane* and *Gladiator* planes were flown aboard the carrier by their pilots to save the aircraft from enemy destruction. They would be needed for protecting the home island. For many of the aviators these were their first carrier landings.[53]

Finding itself low on fuel, the *Glorious* and her two destroyer escorts, *HMS Acasta* and *HMS Ardent*, had been ordered to proceed to England independently. Unbeknownst to them, they were about to encounter the German battleships *Scharnhorst* and

HMS ACASTA in August 1939 - (National Maritime Museum)

Gneisenau which Admiral Raeder had ordered North to attack the evacuating British forces.

The *Glorious* had been built as a light battle cruiser during World War I and converted to an aircraft carrier in 1930. She was fast but ill-equipped to fight a duel with battleships such as the *Scharnhorst* and *Gneisenau*.[54]

Unfortunately, the *Glorious* neglected to maintain an air reconnaissance patrol or a ready strike force with her *Swordfish* aircraft. As a result, she and her escorts were taken by surprise when the *Scharnhorst* opened fire at 28,000 yards. The battleships rained heavy fire on the carrier, its heavy shells ripping into the ship's hangar decks. Although a valiant effort was made by the crew to arm and launch its torpedo bombers, all was in vain. The carrier soon was a mass of flames.

The escorts *Acasta* and *Ardent* closed the mortally wounded ship and laid a smoke screen around it. This did little to stop the carnage and at 5:20 pm the *Glorious* went dead in the water and the order was given to abandon ship. Eight minutes later the gallant *Ardent*, its torpedoes expended, was devastated by enemy gunfire and sent to the bottom.

At 5:40 pm the *Glorious* capsized and sank. Now, only the *Acasta* was left to carry the fight to the enemy. She bravely sailed directly at the enemy ships with all guns blazing while firing a salvo of torpedoes, one of which hit the *Scharnhorst* abeam of her after turret and severely damaged her. However, within a short while the badly damaged destroyer was overwhelmed and sinking.[55]

Aside from the loss of one of the few British aircraft carriers in operation at the time, the loss in men and aircraft was tragic. All but 43 ship's company, naval pilots, observers, and the Royal Air Force crews recently flown aboard were lost. Two men survived the *Ardent*; Leading Seaman G. Carter, RN, was the only survivor of the *Acasta*. Seaman Carter remembered the fierce battle and the final moments of his ship in his official statement to Royal Navy officials.[56]

> "On board our ship, what a deadly calm, hardly a word spoken, the ship was now steaming at full speed away

from the enemy. Then a host of orders. Prepare all smoke floats, hose-pipes connected up, various other jobs were prepared, we were stealing away from the enemy, and making smoke. All our smoke floats had been set going.

"The Captain then had this message passed to all positions: 'You may all think that we are running away from the enemy. We are not. Our chummy ship, *Ardent,* has been sunk and the *Glorious* is sinking.' We then altered course into our smoke-screen. I had the order to stand by to fire tubes six and seven. We came out of the smoke-screen and altered course to starboard firing our torpedoes from the port side. It was then that I had my first glance at the enemy. To be honest, it appeared to me to be a large one and a small one, and we were very close. I fired two torpedoes from my tubes and the foremost tubes fired theirs. We were all watching the results. I'll never forget the cheer that went up as on the port bow of one of the ships a yellow flash and a great column of smoke and water shot up from her. We knew that we had a hit. Personally, I could not see how we could have missed as we were so close.

"The enemy never fired a shot at us, I feel that they must have been very surprised. After we had fired our torpedoes we went back into our own smoke-screen altering course again to starboard. 'Stand by to fire remaining torpedoes!' But this time as soon as we poked our nose out of the smoke-screen, the enemy let us have it. A shell hit the engine-room killing my tube's crew. I was blown to the after end of the tubes. I must have been knocked out for a while, because when I came to, my arm hurt me; the ship had stopped with a list to port. Here is something, believe it or not, I climbed back into the control seat and saw those two ships. I fired the remaining torpedoes, no one told me to, I guess I was raving mad. God alone knows why I fired them but I did.

"The *Acasta*'s guns were firing all the time, even firing with a list on the ship. The enemy then hit us several times and one big explosion took place aft. I have often wondered whether the enemy hit us with a torpedo, in any case it seemed to lift the ship out of the water.

"At last the Captain gave the order to 'Abandon ship.' I will always remember Surgeon Lieutenant H.J. Stammers RNVR, it was his first ship and also his first action. Before jumping over the side I saw him still attending the wounded. A hopeless task. When I was in the water I saw the Captain leaning over the bridge, take a cigarette out of a case and light it. We shouted to him to come to our raft, he waved and called out, 'Goodbye and good luck!' The end of a very gallant man."

Bootsmaat Gunther Schmidt, sole survivor of U-533 (second from right) - (U-Boot Archiv, Cuxhaven)

The Liberty Ship SS PETER SYLVESTER, was torpedoed by U-862 on February 6, 1945 some 7 miles west of Perth, Australia while enroute alone from Melbourne, Australia, to Colombo, Ceyl with cargo of U.S. Army supplies and 317 Army mules carries in stalls on the forward and af decks. Her complement was 42 crew members, 26 Naval Armed Guard, and 106 U.S. Ar personnel. Of this number, one crew member, seven Armed Guard, and 24 Army personnel w lost, a minimal number when one considers the fact that due to the ship's inability to broadcas subarine alarm message, there was a three day delay in the search for survivors. - (Victor C. W Collection)

CHAPTER
EIGHTEEN

THE MONSOON BOATS

On February 6, 1945, the American troopship *SS Peter Sylvester* was sent to the bottom by the German U-boat, *U-862*, some 700 miles west of Perth, Australia. The sinking signalled the end of German submarine war patrols in the Far East. When Germany surrendered 3 months later, six U-boats lay in Far East ports. According to terms agreed to by the Axis powers early in the war, the boats were promptly taken over by the Japanese who interned the crews.[57]

German U-boats first rounded the Cape of Good Hope in late June 1942. Italy, Germany and Japan agreed in December of 1941 to a line of demarcation in assigning Far East submarine operations, e.g., the 70th meridian of East longitude (west of Bombay, the Laccadive Islands, the Maldives, and southward through Kerguelen). Germany and Italy would confine their activity west of this line while the Japanese would run submarine patrols east into the Pacific.

Some 57 U-boats ranged into the Indian Ocean and Pacific waters during the war. The initial group of four 740-ton boats called *Eisbar* or *Polar Bear* departed French bases for Cape Town in August 1942. One of the group, *U-156,* was lost enroute. The remaining force, joined by the first of the new long range *TYPE IXD* boats, achieved remarkable success. During October 1942, *Eisbar* boats sank 24 Allied ships totalling 163,000 gross tons.

The next group called *Kap U-Boote* or *Cape U-Boats* was dispatched southward by Admiral Dönitz in September of 1942 while the *Eisbar* group was still enroute to Cape Town. This group subsequently operated off the Cape and northward into Mozambique Channel. Operating practically unopposed, *Cape U-Boats* sank 36 merchant ships sailing independently during the last 3 months of the year. All U-boats of this group returned safely to their home bases.

The *Seehund* or *Seal* force led by *U-182* Commander Nicolai Clausen sailed into Far East waters in early 1943. Clausen's group included five U-boats and five Italian submarines. Another 24 ships were destroyed by this mixed force. Clausen and Italian Commander Grazzana were credited with the majority of the kills. While homeward bound, *U-182* was depth charged and sunk by U.S. escort destroyers *Mackenzie (DD-614)* and *Laub (DD-613)* some 200 miles WNW of Funchal in the Madeira Islands. Clausen and his entire crew were lost in the action.

In March of 1943 a new group of U-boats arrived in the western Indian Ocean. Although the boats sank 34 merchantmen in a 3-month period, Allied convoys were sighted for the first time. This late arriving tactic along with strengthened antisubmarine forces began to take their toll on patrolling U-boats.

Among this group of U-boat commanders was Fregattenkapitän Wolfgang Lüth, one of Germany's most accomplished submariners. Lüth completed the longest continuous war patrol in submarine history (211 days) during this sortie. Following the patrol during which he added ten ships to his record, he received the Swords and Diamonds to the Oak Leaves Award, worn with the Knight's Cross. He was the seventh man to receive this decoration and the first member of the Navy. As this group departed from the area, one boat, *U-178*, proceeded to Penang, an island off the Malaya Peninsula, to establish a German submarine operating base.

By June of 1943, the "happy days" of Western and Mid-Atlantic U-boat operations were over. U-boat losses mounted as Allied convoy systems and techniques were improved and new *Hunter-Killer* antisubmarine groups roamed the ocean freely in search of their underseas enemy. Between January and July of 1943, 130 U-boats went to the bottom, more than half of the total U-boat operating force.

Dönitz began to look for new areas of operation where Allied shipping remained relatively undefended. Early Indian Ocean operations had reaped an impressive harvest. Between September 1942 and July 1943, U-boats claimed 116 ships for 600,000 gross tons with only three U-boats lost.

Dönitz, Commander-in-Chief of the German Navy in 1943, and his new U-boat Chief, Admiral Hans-Georg von Friedeburg, faced other problems in the Far East that further directed their attention toward increased U-boat activity in that area. German blockade runners that moved critical war materials between Japan and Germany were being lost to British air and naval forces at an alarming rate. The U-boat headquarters staff was convinced that U-boats could readily assume the transporting of vital goods. *TYPE X-B* and *TYPE XIV* cargo carrier U-boats were available along with a number of *TYPE IX-D* boats which were rapidly joining the operational fleet in 1943. These 1,600-ton boats had a surface operational radius of 23,700 miles. Additionally, the Japanese had opened their bases at Penang, Singapore, and Batavia (later renamed Djakarta) to German U-boats.

A plan was developed by the U-boat operational staff that would send large U-boat patrollers (*IX-C* & *IX-D*) and transporters (*VII-F, X-B,* & *XIV*) to the Far East for extensive operations. Groups of boats would proceed to the Indian Ocean independently. Round trip missions would include refueling from U-tankers in the Atlantic and surface ships in the Indian Ocean, war patrols in assigned areas, then in-port periods at Far East bases for repair, overhaul, and crew rest. The boats would then either sortie out on another patrol or take on a vital cargo of tungsten, rubber, tin, quinine, opium, and molybdenum, and head for home waters. The operational schedule called for a continuous stream of boats moving to and from the Far East.

The *Monsoon* campaign commenced in June of 1943 with the departure of 11 U-boats from Norwegian, French, and German bases. The group met almost immediately with fierce enemy opposition. On June 24, *U-200* was sunk by *VP-84 PBY-5A* aircraft south of Iceland. U-tankers *U-462* and *U-514* were sent to the bottom the following month by British air patrols in the Bay of Biscay. U.S. Army Corps *Liberators* destroyed *U-506* west of Vigo, Spain on July 12. And finally, American *Hunter-Killer* antisubmarine groups which included the carriers *Card, Core,* and *Santee* claimed *U-487, U-509,* and *U-847* as they were transiting the Atlantic. *U-509* and *U-847* were lost with all hands.

Of the original 11 *Monsoon* boats, five made it into the Indian Ocean. One of the five, *U-533,* was lost to an obsolete British aircraft flying out of the British base at Sharjah. *U-533* was only on its second patrol. One man was to survive the attack, Bootsmaat Gunther Schmidt.

U-533 was built at Deutsche Werft in Hamburg and launched on 11 September 1942. "Plank Owner" command of the *Type IXC-40* was given to Oberleutnant zur See Helmut Henning. The U-boat was commissioned at Stettin on 25 November 1942 and ordered to Lorient, France to join the 10th U-Flotilla under Chief Korvettenkapitän Kuhnke.

U-533 was ordered out on its first patrol in Group "Star" which was directed to attack Convoy ONS.5. A savage battle ensued with heavy losses to both sides. On 5 May the U-boat was rammed and severely damaged by the British corvette *HMS Sunflower*. All torpedo tubes were put out of commission and the boat barely made it back to Lorient. After extensive repairs, she was made combat ready again and sailed from Lorient on 6 July 1943 on her second and final patrol.

As a part of Group *Monsoon, U-533* successfully entered the Indian Ocean where it reported a number of unsuccessful attacks in September, both in the Gulf of Aden and the Gulf of Oman in the Persian Gulf.

A month later *U-533* continued to operate in the Gulf of Oman and was caught by surprise on the 16th of October by RAF Sergeant L. Chapmanno flying a Blenheim *Bisley* of RAF Squadron 244. Although the aircraft were considered obsolete for their anti-submarine patrol work, the pilots were nevertheless dedicated to their mission. Chapmanno got lucky for on that fateful day he was suddenly surprised to sight a surfaced U-boat below him.

Spotting the oncoming enemy aircraft, Henning immediately dove, but his dive was too slow. This could have been attributed to the fact that he had taken on board many new crew replacements before leaving on the patrol. The attacking aircraft dropped four depth charges as the stern of the U-boat was still above water. Coming about, Chapmanno saw an oil patch, some bubbles, and scattered debris in the water. He reported the attack and sinking when he returned to base that evening. The next day a search was made of the area with negative results.

Bootsmaat Gunther Schmidt and the 1st Watch Officer, Lt. z. S. Paasehen, stood near a hatch that blew open when the U-boat was sinking; both were blown out by the boat's pressure when it became unseated. When Schmidt swam over to the officer he saw that he was unconscious. Alone, in the warm seas and with no life jackets, Schmidt held the officer up for over an hour until his strength gave out and the officer slipped away. Schmidt started swimming west under the merciless sun. After 28 torturous hours in the water he made landfall on the Arabian coast and was nursed back to health by friendly Arabs. Wanting to help him further, they sought assistance at a nearby British base which turned out to be the home field for RAF Squadron 244. Four days later a British patrol came for him and took him to the base at Sharjah as a prisoner-of-war.

During his interrogation he told his captors that many of the men on the U-boat were not trained and were new replacements. He talked further about the experiences of his boat and crew.

> "On our way out one destroyer depth charged us the whole night, always at short intervals. The W/T

(wireless telegraph/radio) operator kept reporting, destroyer coming nearer, and right over us. Whenever she was straight above, the Captain proceeded at maximum or 3/4 speed. He would turn off our engines and then turn them back on to silent running. If she was right over us she couldn't hear us due to her own propeller noises. The search gear made sort of a singing noise which is always deceptive when it sings like that.

"We sweated blood that night. How it rumbled, and we were at a depth of 180 meters too. Finally, when we got through to the Gulf of Aden, the officer of the watch said, 'I feel like a new man now!' Even he had never experienced anything like that; he too, had sweated blood. He thought it was the end of us. Nearly all the lights were smashed which had never actually happened to us before, although on the first patrol, all six torpedo tubes were put out of action. All the upper deck torpedoes were smashed and all tubes bent."

Gunther Schmidt also claimed that the *U-533* had made some landings ashore and purchased items from the natives.

321
321

CHAPTER
NINETEEN

WARRANT OFFICER KARL WISNIEWSKI

U.S.S. Besugo (SS321), Report of Fourth War Patrol[58]
23 April 1945

0400(I)	Arrived on station.
0505(I)	Dove to flush out tank. Surfaced at 0542(I), patrolling north and south on station.
0731(I)	Dived for submerged patrol during day.
1200(I)	Position 04.56S / 112.52E.
1350(I)	Sighted submarine bearing 262 (True), commenced submerged approach. Target zigging radically about 50 each side of base course 085 (True), making 10 knots over the ground. Turn count 240 RPM.
1414(I)	Identified submarine as German with Japanese merchant flag painted on upper side of conning tower and flying enormous Japanese warship colors.

USS BESUGO (SS-321) circa the mid-1950's - (U.S. Naval Historical Center)

1427-29(I) Commenced firing spread of 6 Mk. 18 torpedoes, set depth 8 feet. Range 1500 yds., speed 10, angle on bow 90 Port.

1429(I) One hit. Looked no more than 4 seconds later, but sub had disappeared. Nothing visible but smoke, a slick of air bubbles and the beginning of an oil slick, 04.56S / 112.55E.

1436(I) Surfaced to recover survivors.

1440(I) Rescued German war prisoner Warrant Officer Karl Wisniewski, #UN2101/343, German Navy who had been navigator of the sunken submarine and who identified her as the *U-183*, of 740 ton class. He was the only survivor in the large oil slick and was treated for the following injuries: dislocated left knee, broken right collar bone, lacerated bridge of nose, lacerated lips and mouth, and three missing teeth.

The sinking of *U-183* in the Java Sea marked the sudden end to Germany's first attempt to disrupt American naval operations in the Pacific. Under command of Kapitänleutnant Fritz Schneewind, the U-boat had departed Batavia (Djakarta), Djawa for patrol off the Philippines. She suffered the dubious honor of being the second German U-boat to be sunk by American submarines and was the last of the German Far East boats to be lost in the war.

The following account is Warrant Officer Wisniewski's recollection of the final patrol and sinking.

> "*U-183* left the port of Batavia at dusk on April 21, 1945 without attracting attention. Our conning tower was marked on both sides with the color of the Japanese flag as a security against the Japanese army. We soon left the minefields behind and headed into the Java Sea.
>
> "A sharp lookout was ordered for any sea targets and our radio operator kept a tuned ear for possible radar contacts. Nothing happened during the night hours. With the new day a Japanese aircraft patrolled overhead and we were all happy about this precaution

taken by our allies. The watchmen on the bridge had to look out mainly for enemy submarines which had proven troublesome in this area. We set a zigzag course to counter any attack from an unseen enemy.

''Nothing worth mentioning happened this day and the following night. The next morning, April 23rd, we headed east towards the Makassar Strait. Our Japanese reconnaissance aircraft had departed and we were left alone to make our way through the shimmering waters of the Java Sea south of Borneo where Australian troops were landing at the time.

''At noon the crew on the bridge changed shifts and the commander assumed his position at the helm. Again they watched for enemy submarines but didn't sight anything. At 1320 hours the commander left the bridge. His last orders were, 'normal watch.' That meant that the airspace should also be observed and we should dive if anything was sighted.The officer who took over the shift with six experienced watchmen checked the airspace immediately for aircraft and when he put down his binoculars and looked to the watchpost a large explosion occurred. A five meter jet of flame came up on the port side of the bridge and the boat shuddered. With pain racked faces the watchmen fell from their positions and a single scream came out of the boat as water streamed in. That was the end, in a matter of a few seconds. Still doing top speed the boat sunk fast. Having been at the helmsman's position I was able to swim to the surface again and waited for one of my comrades to appear, but I was alone in the middle of the oil slick. Not knowing what happened, I hoped that if it had been a torpedo the enemy submarine would surface and save me.

''But there was only the play of the waves while blood, mixed with the thick black oil slick, covered the sea. I was suddenly aware that my leg had been injured. I felt my energy beginning to fade and I knew that only fast help could save me. I tried to hold on as long as I could and hoped for rescue.

"After about ten minutes time a submarine surfaced, sped up and headed towards me. After picking me up they searched for more than an hour for more survivors but none were sighted. The water covered *U-Schneewind*, which was laying on the bottom some 65 meters below. Fifty-four of my comrades were lost in the ill-fated boat.

"The submarine that surfaced weighed 2,000 tons, was American and commanded by Commander Miller. The boat did test dives that morning 80 nautical miles west of the Boef Islands. Before surfacing, the periscope was raised and the area checked. Then a ship was noticed at about 14,000 yards which they thought was a sailboat. After that they heard propeller noises. It was clear to them then that it was a submarine whose bridge looked like a sail. Because our boat was heading right towards them they had nothing to do except wait until it was in position whereupon they fired a fan of six torpedoes at us. I found this out during the four weeks I was aboard the submarine while it conducted operations."

During his stay on the *Besugo,* Wisniewski was treated for his injuries although he succeeded in misaligning his right clavicle after it was lined up properly. The *Besugo* log states that Wisniewski was an uncooperative patient and desired much special care, which he did not get. He was quite unpopular until he became semi-ambulatory.

The *Besugo* returned from patrol on 20 May 1945, mooring alongside the *U.S.S. Anthedon* at Subic Bay in the Philippines. Wisniewski was taken to the 126th General Hospital where he was further treated for his injuries. He was interrogated prior to being transferred to the hospital and again while recovering. He gave little operational information to his interrogators. His personal history, however, appeared to be fairly accurate.

He was born in Cologne in December of 1915. At the age of 17 he was expelled from Baker Apprentice School for saying that the Russian Communist government would last more than 2 years. He tried to become a policeman in 1933, but was thwarted because he was not a party member. Wisniewski joined the Navy in 1933 and spent 1940-1941 on the German auxiliary cruiser *Thor* in the South Atlantic. He later spent 2 years as Commanding Officer of a patrol craft in the English Channel before being ordered to Bordeaux and duty on board the *U-183*.

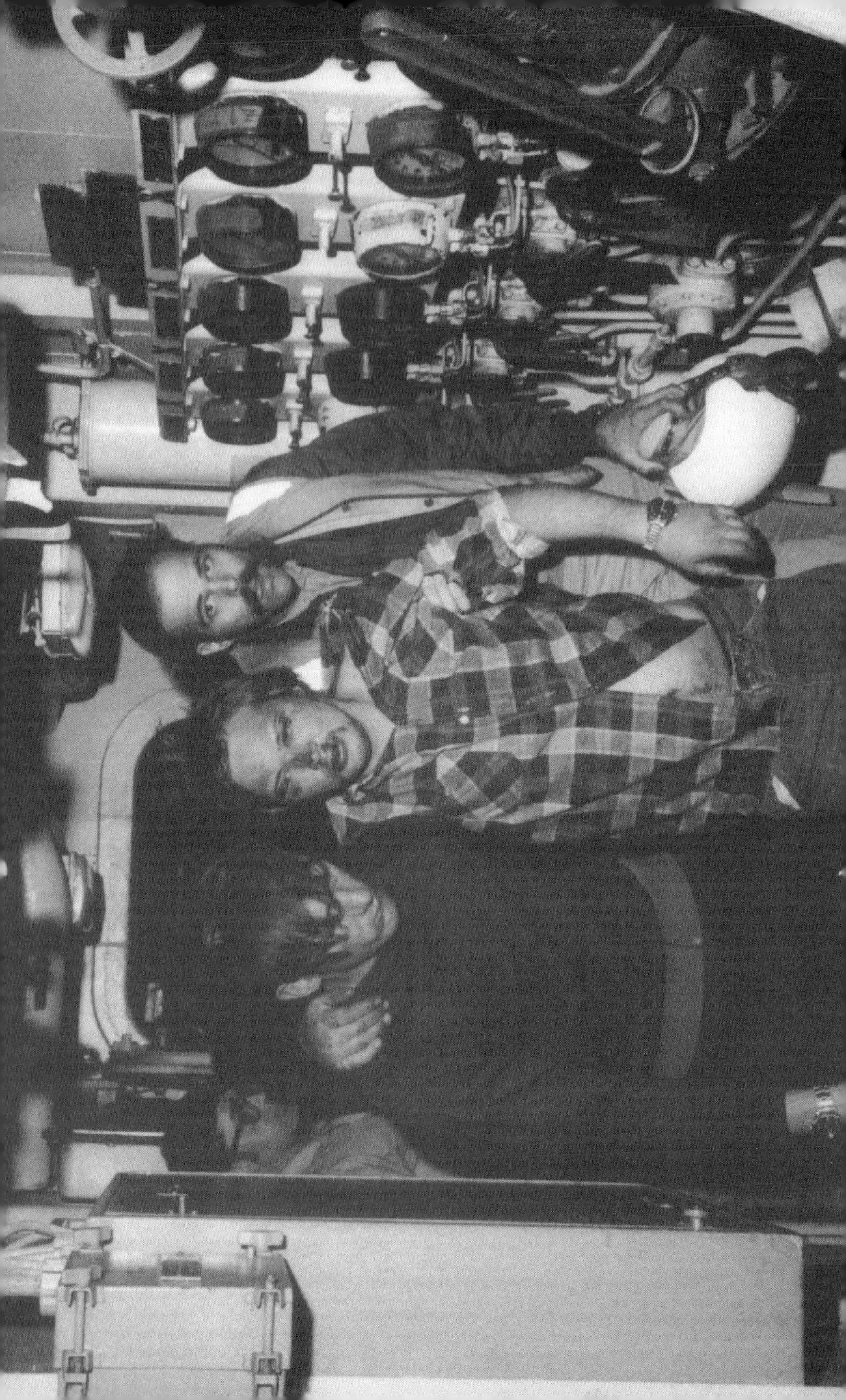

CHAPTER TWENTY

KILLER SEAS

Most of the sole survivor stories in this book deal with incidents of war which caused enormous losses in ships and men. Even when crews were able to abandon ship in lifeboats or rafts, the fury of seas whipped by frigid storms and hurricane-like winds doomed them before they could be rescued or make it safely to some distant shore. The few who survived in these instances made it back through sheer individual perseverance and luck.

Quite often the sea would strike without warning. On October 23, 1941, *U-106*, under the command of Kapitänleutnant Herman Rasch, lost an entire bridge watch due to heavy seas. Headquarters could only assume that a series of huge swells had overtaken the boat and the watchstanders, not strapped in at their posts, had been washed overboard.[59]

Since the end of World War II, many vessels have succumbed to angry seas and gone to the bottom. Such was the case of the Norwegian Freighter *Norse Variant* on March 22, 1973. The *Norse*

Norwegian merchant seaman Stein Gabrielson from Oslo, Norway, the sole survivor of his ship, is being escorted to sickbay on board the attack aircraft carrier USS INDEPENDENCE. Gabrielson was rescued from the water by a U.S. Coast Guard helicopter. - (Naval Photographic Center)

Variant incident is included in this chronicle because one man survived the ordeal, ship's mechanic Stein Gabrielsen.[60]

The 541-foot, 12,946-ton freighter, owned by Odd Codager of Oslo, Norway, departed Norfolk, Virginia on March 21, 1973 bound for Glasgow, Scotland. Laden with a cargo of Appalachian coal, the ship sailed into a heavy sea and dark overcast sky. Since the *Norse Variant* had withstood the worst the Atlantic could offer in the past, the crew was confident that the journey would be without incident. It was wintertime and heavy weather was expected.

The following morning the ship and crew faced a worsening situation. Heavy winds blew from the north across the wind-streaked water as huge waves crashed against the ship. About mid-morning a thunderous wave exploded over the bow and crashed onto the forward hatch, breaking it open. Water began rushing into the ship and although the ship's pumps appeared to be handling the situation, the ship's master, Captain Jens-Otto Harsem, decided to turn about and head back to Norfolk for repairs. A few hours later another wave struck with devastating effect. The forward crane was stripped of its deck welding and the No. 2 hold opened to the seas now engulfing the forward part of the ship. Slowly, the ship settled by the bow as it began to break apart. Captain Harsem knew that his ship was doomed. He signalled the lifeboat alarm at approximately 1:45 p.m.

Stein Gabrielsen fastened on his life jacket as he rushed to the afterdeck. There the captain ordered that the life rafts be hurled into the sea and the crew abandon ship immediately. He informed them that the ship's radio officer had signalled their situation to the U.S. Coast Guard and help would soon be on the way. (The ship had in fact sent its first distress signal at 12:28 p.m. reporting its position as 150 miles southeast of Cape May.) Two more huge breakers crashed over the ship and in a matter of seconds the *Norse Variant* slid under the boiling sea.

Stein suddenly found himself underwater being pulled down by the suction of the sinking ship. Struggling desperately, he gradually loosened himself from the watery death grip and fought his way to the surface. The water was bitter cold as he rode up and down on the massive waves. He suddenly sighted a raft and swam to it, pulling himself aboard. He scanned the seas around him for other survivors. He sighted two other crewmen in the water but was unable to reach them.

Meanwhile the Coast Guard Rescue Coordination Center on Governors' Island, New York, began coordination of the *Norse Variant* search effort. At one time or another during the next three days the cutters *Dallas, Tamaroa, Cherokee, Gresham, Firebrush,* and *Spencer;* the Navy submarine rescue ship *Kittiwake;* oiler *Caloosahatchee;* the attack carrier *Independence; HC-130*s flying out of Pease and Elgin AFB, Florida and Coast Guard Air Station Elizabeth City, North Carolina, and two *HH-3F*s out of Coast Guard Air Station, Brooklyn, New York took part in the operation.

While search operations went into high gear, Stein frantically clung to ropes inside the raft which was being buffeted by hurricane force winds. Sleet and snow whipped his body as he rode sea swells which rose as high as 40 feet. In an instant a crashing breaker drove him deep beneath the sea. Using every ounce of strength, he finally fought his way to the surface leaving his raft far below, torn by the treacherous currents.

Stein kept thinking to himself that the Coast Guard would soon find him; it would only be a matter of hours. He rode the high crest of the waves searching the sea for something to cling to. The impossible happened, another raft came into view a few hundred yards away. He fought his way to the bright orange, square shaped craft and struggled aboard. This time he tied the raft's lifeline around his arm.

That night he heard a plane roar overhead and although he was able to fire off two flares, the aircraft continued on course unaware of the lone man below. Toward the middle of the night searchlights swept through the wind driven seas from a ship less than a quarter of a mile away. Stein waved his arms and shouted to his would-be rescuers. The wailing wind and poor visibility offered little hope of his being seen or heard.

As dawn came on March 23, Stein could no longer feel his feet, which had turned blue. He knew that he must revive circulation in his legs if he was to survive. He climbed over the side and kicked his legs until he felt some warmth return to his frigid body. However, once back in the raft the sea rose up once again and capsized the raft pinning him underneath. Through frantic maneuvering he squeezed himself along the underside of the raft and popped out onto the surface. Later that afternoon another huge wave threw him from the raft and he barely made it back aboard. Battered and bruised, he hung on, refusing to give up. He forced himself to remain awake, thinking to himself that if he could last one more day, help would come.

By Saturday morning the winter storm had run its course and Stein now stared out at an empty sea, completely exhausted. Unbeknownst to him was the massive search and rescue operation going on at that moment. Planes and ships were searching a 12,600-square-mile grid area looking for any sign of the *Norse Variant* and a sister ship *Anita* which had also disappeared in the storm. Stein remained awake through the night and amidst calm seas the following morning he finally fell asleep. He had drifted 120 miles southeast of where the *Norse Variant* had gone down.

That morning Lieutenant Commander Edward L. Weilbacher, a Coast Guard veteran, lifted his Air Force *HC-130* from Pease Air Force Base at 5:10 a.m. An hour later he and his crew arrived at the search area and began their patrol. Weather conditions were such that there was little hope of finding survivors of the lost ships.

About an hour into the search, Commander Weilbacher recalled, they began to see a driftline of debris on the surface of the sea—life jackets, flotsam, a small rubber life raft, and a larger one. All were empty, and there was no sign of life.

Shortly after 9 a.m., Lieutenant Ronald Balleu, the co-pilot, saw an orange raft about a mile from the search track. "It was a type I'd never seen before, square and very large," Commander Weilbacher remembered.

Weilbacher maneuvered his aircraft over the raft and there, much to his surprise, was a man kneeling in the center. "We circled him a few times and he was waving and jumping." Weilbacher could not imagine how the man survived in those sea conditions.

Weilbacher reported the position back to base and then flew toward the *Mobile Lube,* a 617-foot tanker of the Mobil Oil Corporation, which was 15 miles away. Radio contact was impossible, so Weilbacher laid down white smoke floats near the raft and then buzzed across the tanker's bow to try to divert it. The loadmaster of the plane flashed an SOS from the cargo door of the plane.

Not seeing any response, Weilbacher returned to the raft. This time, the men noticed a pile of what appeared to be blankets in the raft and thought it might be another survivor in need of medical assistance. Weilbacher decided to deploy his pararescue team. T. Sergeant Roy A. Taylor, a Vietnam veteran, and Sargeant Rickey J. Cofer, wearing scuba gear and carrying a radio and medical kit, parachuted from 1,000 feet.

The two men dropped almost on top of the raft. Taylor and Cofer ditched their chutes in the water and swam a few feet to the raft. At 10:22 a.m. the rescue team reported that Stein was in good condition. His first question to his rescuers when they climbed on to the raft was, ''Have you found any others?'' Hearing that he was the lone survivor, he closed his eyes and went limp.

By now, the *Mobile Lube* had finally received word of the situation and turned toward the raft. After careful maneuvering in deep swells, the tanker put out a life boat and recovered Stein and the pararescue team. Later, a Coast Guard helicopter transferred Stein to the *Independence* where he was thoroughly examined by the ship's medical team. Amazingly, Stein was found to be only slightly dehydrated and suffering from cuts and bruises. During his 70 hours of turmoil he had survived hurricane force winds, mountainous seas, and near-freezing nights. He was able to walk with assistance once on board the *Independence.*

Not in need of hospitalization, Stein was later taken to the Norwegian Consulate in New York and then transported back to Norway to rejoin his family.

Stein's rescuers called his survival a ''one in a million'' sighting, considering the weather conditions and inherent difficulties air search crews encounter in finding someone lost at sea. The event of his rescue and good physical condition after such a harrowing experience can only be described as some kind of "miracle" that happens now and then to those who ply the seas.

CHAPTER
TWENTY ONE

LIVORNO DISASTER

It should have been a routine cruise for crewman Alessio Bertrand. He and his comrades watched a European soccer match as his ship, the car ferry *Moby Prince,* began its 10-hour night journey from Leghorn, Italy to the port city of Olbia on the island of Sardinia on April 11, 1991. The ferry carried 76 passengers and a crew of 63.[61]

Suddenly, a thick fog covered the water and as the ferry reached a point 3 miles from Leghorn, disaster struck. Unseen by the ferry crew and missed on the ship's radar screen was the anchored supertanker, *Agip Abruzzo,* which lay directly in its path.

The two ships collided and were immediately engulfed in flames as crude oil burst from a hole in the side of the tanker. The skipper of the *Abruzzo,* Captain Renato Superina, stated that, "We heard a tremendous explosion . . . the flames flared up immediately. We stayed on board trying to put them out for as long as we could stand it, but after a short while we had to abandon

Tugboats surround jthe MOBY PRINCE in the port of Leghorn, Italy after the ferry collided with an oil tanker in thick fog. The ferry MOBY PRINCE was sailing between Olbia, Sardinia to Leghorn when it collided with the oil tanker, leaving 140 people missing - (AP/Wide World Photos)

ship.'' Captain Superina and his entire crew manned the ship's lifeboats and escaped the burning inferno.

On board the ferry there was chaos. Sailor Bertrand told television interviewers later in his hospital room in Leghorn that, ''Smoke and flames were everywhere. We couldn't jump into the sea because that too was on fire. My mates hung on as long as they could, but one by one they collapsed.'' Bertrand hung on to the ship's railing for 2 hours until rescued. He was the sole survivor aboard the *Moby Prince*. ''I'm not a hero,'' he said. ''I saw people on the ground, paralyzed, dead. Some had died of suffocation. Some were completely charred . . . I walked over corpses . . . It's a miracle that I'm alive.''

CHAPTER
TWENTY TWO

OFFICIAL SOLE SURVIVOR INCIDENT REPORTS

TOLTEN (Chile)
S.S. ATLANTIC SUN (U.S.)
S.S. W.D. ANDERSON (U.S.)
S.S. PUERTO RICAN (U.S.)
U-68 (Germany)
U-378 (Germany)
U-413 (Germany)
U-419 (Germany)
U-1199 (Germany)
I-365 (Japan)
I-373 (Japan)

SS TOLTEN - *(Steamship Historical Society of America, Inc.)*

Freighter *TOLTEN* (Chile)

Navy Department

Office of the Chief of Naval Operations

Washington

OP-16-B-5 March 27, 1942

MEMORANDUM FOR FILE

Subject: Summary of Statements by the Lone Survivor, Chilean Freighter, *TOLTEN*.

1. The *TOLTEN* was torpedoed without warning during the night of March 14, 1942, time unknown while located approximately 30 miles south of Ambrose. The *TOLTEN* was proceeding northward with Chilean flag flying and Chilean flag painted on hull. Lights were on until about 3 hours prior to the attack when a vessel approached and ordered in English that the lights be extinguished. The lone survivor jumped overboard immediately following the explosion and reports the vessel blew up within 5 minutes. From 16 to 21 persons were aboard. The submarine was not seen.

A.J. Powers
Ensign, U.S.N.R.

(Author's Note: Built in 1904, *Tolten* was owned by Trinder, Anderson & Company, an Australian Steam Shipping Company. The ship was sunk by *U-404* under the command of Korvettenkapitän Otto N. Bülow, winner of the Knight's Cross with Oak Leaves. A little over a year after sending the *Tolten* to the bottom, *U-404* was one of nine U-boats sunk in what the British command called the "Big Bay (of Biscay) Slaughter." *U-404* was the first to go down, sunk by an Anglo-American *Liberator* team (U.S. Army Antisubmarine Squadron 4 and British Squadron 224). The U-boat was sunk with a loss of all hands.[62]

A thorough search of official records by the author failed to uncover the identity of the *Tolten's* sole survivor.

U-124 crew sank the S.S. ATLANTIC - *(Bundersarchiv)*

S.S. Atlantic Sun (U.S.)

Navy Department

Office of the Chief of Naval Operations

Washington, D.C.

10 March 1945

MEMORANDUM FOR FILE

ALL TIMES GCT

Subject: Summary of Statement by Survivor *M/V ATLANTIC SUN* (U.S.), Tanker, 11,615 tons, owned and operated by the Sun Oil Co.

1. The *ATLANTIC SUN* was torpedoed at about 1300 GCT (Greenwich Civil Time) on 15 February 1943 approximately 150

miles off Cape Race, Newfoundland, having sailed from Reykjavik, Iceland, 7 February 1943, presumably to New York in Convoy ON.165 but at time of attack was travelling independently, with water ballast, amount and distribution of which is unknown, as is the draft of the vessel. Ship was split in two and the fore section settled rapidly at the bridge housing, bow raised above water, and slid under about 20 minutes after torpedoes struck. A third torpedo struck drifting after section about 1530 GCT. The stern settled rapidly, the fore part of the section rose beyond the perpendicular and turned over, leaving the section keel up. It sank entirely about one half hour after torpedo struck.

2. Course of ship unknown, speed estimated at approximately 15 knots, believed zig-zagging. Ship had lost convoy (cause unknown) during the night of 13 February, and was travelling independently. Number of look-outs unknown at time of action. There was a light fog, moderate swells, wind direction unknown, force estimated at 15 knots, visibility about 1/4 mile. No ships in sight.

3. At approximately 1300 something struck the ship which felt like a very heavy sea with a muffled roar. Apparently two torpedoes had struck on the port side one splitting the vessel in half just aft of the midship housing at about the pumproom, and one causing a large hole in the bow at the forefoot. The engines in the aft section were stopped. The fore section of the vessel was about 50 yards distance and sinking. As the Master, Radio Operator, and Armed Guard Officer were in the midships area of the fore section, there is no knowledge of codes, radio damage, distress signals, etc. The drifting aft section was examined for damage, and, as it was not taking water, and engines appeared to be in order, it was believed it could be maneuvered to a port. At approximately 1530 the track of a third torpedo was seen approaching the aft section about 20 yards distant on the port side aft. It struck about 15 feet forward of the stern post, and apparently caused a large hole. No column of water was seen or felt though a muffled roar was heard. There was no smoke or flame. Stern sank at about 1600. Confidential codes went down with the forward section.

4. At approximately 1310 after the first two torpedoes struck, the starboard lifeboat from the aft section of the vessel was launched with approximately 22 men in charge of the Chief Officer. At approximately 1500 this boat returned to the floating aft section. Consuming about 30 minutes reboarding the section by way of nets, the men from the lifeboat then went below to change clothes. At approximately 1530 when the third torpedo struck, these men from the lifeboat were still below. A port lifeboat was launched with approximately eight men in it. Four men went over the starboard side into the sea. One survivor was picked up by a German submarine and carried to St. Nazaire, France, 9 March 1943. The lifeboat, half swamped, with approximately eight men, was left adrift by the submarine. Total complement aboard 66, including 46 merchant crew, 19 Armed Guard and one passenger. There is one known survivor.
5. About 20 minutes after third torpedo struck sub surfaced about 25 yards away from the lifeboat. About five men, including officers and ratings appeared on the deck of the sub. One officer, rank unknown, asked in good English the name of the ship and destination. Someone in the lifeboat replied and the sub then departed. About ten minutes later sub returned to the vicinity. The survivor swam over to the sub and was picked up. Shortly thereafter the sub got underway leaving the lifeboat with the eight survivors.

The sub was described as of medium size, tonnage unknown, painted olive green, no streaks or stripes, length about 180′, high steep oblong conning tower with turret aft, one gun forward, one on conning tower turret. Sub had a ballast bulge, jumping wires and no net cutter. Its estimated speed was 16 knots on the surface. There was a crew of about 40. Captain stated that four or five trainees were present.

The survivor indicated that the Captain and officers of the submarine had treated him fairly. The captain told the survivor the approximate location of the attack and that he had missed with one further torpedo. Three officers spoke good English, ages from 22-34. One night rendezvous was made with a surface vessel which gave fuel and provisions to the submarine. One evening while on deck survivor saw several other submarines in the vicinity believed to be part of a wolf pack. One attack was made on another vessel, as survivor, who slept in hammock in torpedo compartment aft, felt explosions in the water outside. The Captain later told survivor they had attacked an English vessel, had missed, and the explosions were from depth charges dropped by aircraft. The submarine had apparently been out since early January 1943 as the crew had been home for Christmas and left soon after. No further successful attacks were made by the sub prior to its arrival at St. Nazaire, France 9 March 1943, from which port the survivor was subsequently transferred to Milag Prison Camp via Wilhelmshaven.

BARBARA CONARD
Lt. (jg) USNR.

(Author's Note: The sole survivor of the *Atlantic Sun*, Ordinary Seaman William Golobich, 23, spent 23 days aboard U-607 before being disembarked at St. Nazaire, France. He spent the next 22 months at Milag Nord, a detention camp for merchant seamen which was located approximately 20 miles northeast of Bremen. Of the 3,000 prisoners there, about 60 were Americans.

On 15 January 1945, Golobich along with most of the other American prisoners were released and sent home via Geneva, Switzerland, and Marseilles, France. At Marseilles, they boarded the motor ship *Gripsholm* and left on 9 February and arrived at New York on 21 February.

U-607 sunk five ships (44,138 GRT) during wartime operations. Two skippers operated the boat during its operational career, e.g., Kapitänleutnant Ernst Mengersen, winner of the Knight's Cross and Kapitänleutnant Jeschonnek.[63]

The veteran boat was sunk 18 July 1943 by British Squadron 228 north of Cape Ortegal, Spain.[64]

SS W.D. ANDERSON - (Steamship Historical Society of America, Inc.)

S.S. W.D. Anderson (U.S.)

Navy Department

Office of the Chief of Naval Operations

Washington

OP-16-B-5 March 10, 1942

MEMORANDUM FOR FILE

Subject: Summary of Statement by Survivor of *W.D. Anderson*, American Refining Company Tanker

1. The *W.D. Anderson* was torpedoed without warning at 1900 EWT (Eastern War Time), February 22, 1942 when about 12 miles northeast off Jupiter Light, Florida. The lone survivor states that the *W.D. Anderson* was proceeding northward at about 10 or 11 knots with a moderate sea, few white caps, wind believed from northwest, and no lights showing. A dull thud and booming

explosion were heard. Almost instantly a flame 20 to 30 feet high appeared entirely across ship, probably aft of midship. The flame followed the explosion by a few seconds. The survivor dove overboard in a matter of seconds. While he was in the air the second explosion occurred. After being in the water about 2 hours he heard three explosions, about 15 minutes later three more explosions. The ship was seen to settle down to the stack by the survivor. A submarine periscope was sighted by the second mate about 1000 that morning when passing Key West. This was reported by radio. In an hour or so planes circled the ship and left. It is believed by the survivor that the submarine may have trailed the *W.D. Anderson* all day waiting until dusk to attack. The *SS Walter Jennings* which was close behind the *W.D. Anderson* reported hearing a radio conversation between the two submarines in which the statement was made, ''He is next.'' The master of the *SS Walter Jennings* believed this statement referred to his own boat. The survivor was picked up by a small fishing boat and later transferred to a Coast Guard vessel. The latter was chased for 20 to 30 minutes by an unknown vessel which played a searchlight on her. When the Coast Guard vessel stopped and layed to, the unknown craft did likewise.

A.J. Powers
Ensign, U.S.N.R.

(Author's Note: Author was unable to identify the sole survivor following a search of official files and other source materials. The ship was sunk by *U-504* under the command of Fregattenkapitän Fritz Poske, holder of the Knight's Cross. The U-boat was later sunk with all hands on July 30, 1943 by *HMS Kite, HMS Woodpecker, HMS Wren,* and *HMS Wild Goose* northwest of Cape Ortegal, Spain.[65])

U-68 - *(Bibliothek für Zeitgeschichte Stuttgart)*

U-68 on the way to Norge, 1943 - *(Bibliothek für Zeitgeschichte Stuttgart)*

U-68 beside U-141 - *(Bibliothek für Zeitgeschichte Stuttgart)*

S.S. Puerto Rican (U.S.)

Navy Department

Office of the Chief of Naval Operations

Washington, D.C.

May 14, 1943

MEMORANDUM FOR FILE

Subject: Summary of Statement by Survivor of the *SS PUERTO RICAN*, U.S. Cargo Ship, 6076 GCT, owned by Maritime Commission, operated by American Hawaiian SS Co., chartered to War Shipping Administration on Government Service.

1. The *SS PUERTO RICAN* was torpedoed without warning at 2106 GCT on March 9, 1943, at 66.44N / 10.41W, or 287 miles north of Iceland, having sailed from Russia in convoy RA.53 on March 1, 1943 for the United Kingdom with an unknown quantity of ore. Ship sank on an even keel 20 minutes after torpedo struck.

2. Data as to course, speed, zigzagging, blackout, use of radio, and number of lookouts unknown, save that she had straggled from the convoy. Weather overcast with rain and heavy sea. No other ships in sight.

3. At 2106 GCT a torpedo struck the ship aft of #5 hatch. Main engines secured in 5 minutes. Extent of damage unknown except a hole aft where torpedo hit as assessed by survivor. No distress signal sent. Confidentials believed to have sunk with the ship. All other data unknown.

4. Immediately after torpedo struck, the crew attempted to abandon ship in two lifeboats and two liferafts. Both boats overturned while the rafts got away safely. According to the survivor's story, those on the rafts either froze to death or were washed overboard. The sole survivor was picked up by the British destroyer *HMS ELISTIN* March 12th and brought to Seydisfjordur. He was placed aboard the *U.S.S. Gemini* and landed at Reykjavik 1800 March 16th. Merchant crew of the *SS PUERTO RICAN* numbered 38-Armed Guard 24. Lone survivor is in the

SS PUERTO RICAN - (Steamship Historical Society of America, Inc.)

208th Station Hospital, Helgafell, Iceland, undergoing an operation to remove both feet.

5. The submarine was not seen.

6. The survivor feels he owes his life to the rubber suit he was wearing. Others who abandoned ship without this gear froze almost immediately and were washed overboard by the heavy seas. Although this man was on deck at the time the torpedo struck he showed presence of mind enough to go below and don the suit which this officer believes was responsible for his being alive today.

Robert G. Fulton
Lieut. (jg), USNR

(Author's Note: The sole survivor of the *SS Puerto Rican* was Fireman August Wallenhaupt. Correcting the above official report, the young merchant seaman in fact lost both of his legs and all his fingers down to the knuckles, except for the thumb on his right hand and two fingers of his left hand.

When he finally was well enough to leave Iceland for the United States, his weight had dropped from 170 to 87 pounds. Wallenhaupt spent the next eight months in the Marine hospital on Staten Island. During that time his local Marine Union presented him with a pair of aluminum legs. He was soon walking with the help of a cane.

Wallenhaupt subsequently took a desk job with his shipping company and enrolled in general business courses and language training programs. He learned to write legibly, using his thumb and knuckle joint of the index finger. Thus, the spirited 27 year old started life anew showing the same courage and determination he displayed in surviving the sinking of his ship and his long road to recovery.

The *SS Puerto Rican* was one of four ships sunk by *U-586* while under the command of Kapitänleutnant Götze. The U-boat was destroyed at Toulon by U.S. Army Air Force bombers on 5 July 1944.)[66]

USS GUADALCANAL (CVE 60) - (U.S. National Archives)

U-68 (Germany)

O.N.I. (Office of Naval Intelligence) Report of Interrogation: U-68[67]

U-68 left Lorient on 26 March 1944 for her final patrol.

Her officers were:

Commanding Officer	-	Lauzemis
Executive Officer	-	Meyer
II. Watch Officer	-	Oberleutnant z. S. Keller
Engineer Officer	-	Volmari

Tropical kit was stated to have been issued to the crew. *U-68* was escorted by a Sparebreaker (barrier-breaking vessel; auxiliary minesweeper) and a minesweeper into the Bay of Biscay; the original escort broke off in the bay and a destroyer came up to remain with the U-boat until Cape Finisterre was passed.

Approximately 12 hours after the destroyer put about, *U-68* was attacked by a twin-engined aircraft. She fought the plane off with her guns and was not damaged. (O.N.I. Note: There is no record of a comparable attack in this area at this time.)

The sole survivor stated that there were no further attacks on or by *U-68* prior to the action which led to her sinking. She proceeded toward the South Atlantic and was stated to have been on course 210 degrees for 48 hours prior to the final action.

The survivor maintained that, 3 days before *U-68* was sunk, Control had radioed that an American escort carrier was in her immediate vicinity. The carrier was described as a 12,000 ton ship, with a complement of 1100 men and an escort of four destroyers.

During the night of 9/10 April, the survivor was off watch and asleep in the forward torpedo compartment. He was awakened by the sound of distant depth charge explosions which were attributed to an attack on another U-boat in the area. In this connection, the survivor stated that a "number" of U-boats were operating nearby. (O.N.I. Note: Aircraft VT-30 from *U.S.S. Guadalcanal* sighted a surfaced U-boat at 0359 GCT on 10 April in position 33.40 N / 18.39 W and attacked with rockets and depth bombs. Result of this attack was inconclusive, but it is believed that the boat attacked was not *U-68*.)

The survivor stated that *U-68* was proceeding fully surfaced early on the morning of 10 April when a lookout reported the approach of enemy aircraft. The deck guns were ordered manned and the survivor took his station at the 3.7 cm. gun, which he served. In the ensuing action, 200 rounds were fired from this gun but, in the general confusion, the survivor could not ascertain what damage was done to the U-boat or to the planes.

He recalled four distinct attacks, a strafing run from astern followed by a depth charge attack, the bombs falling close aboard to port slightly abaft the conning tower, another run astern, and an attack by a plane crossing the U-boat from the starboard beam. He did not know how many planes attacked *U-68* at this time. Suddenly, the siren was sounded for a crash dive. The survivor helped secure the 3.7 cm. gun and then noticed that one of the gunners had been wounded. He struggled forward with the wounded man, attempting to bring him into the boat.

As they approached the conning tower hatch, it was slammed shut and the U-boat began to submerge. In a moment, the two men were in the water, pulled under by the suction, but clear of the U-boat. The survivor, whose life jacket had been punctured by bullets and was comparatively ineffective, remained with the wounded man for some time. The latter, wounded in the stomach and leg, had turned very pale and was unconscious. The sole survivor stated that two planes came over after he had been in the water a few minutes and dropped more depth charges; finally, one of the planes dropped a rubber boat. The survivor lost consciousness shortly thereafter from the effort of supporting himself and the wounded man in the water.

(O.N.I. Note: Following is a digest of the action reported by the attacking aircraft.)

At 0626 GCT, 10 April, aircraft *VT-24* from *U.S.S. Guadalcanal*, searching in the area of the contact made by plane *VT-30* earlier in the morning, sighted a U-boat in position 33.25 N / 18.59 W. The U-boat, observed in moonlight fully surfaced, opened fire during the plane's approach for a rocket attack. Eight rockets were fired in four bursts of two rockets each. The pilot reported several direct hits, but could not observe damage to the U-boat. Circling to the left after the rocket attack, *VT-24* delivered a depth bomb attack from the U-boat's starboard quarter, through heavy A/A (AntiAircraft) fire. Two Mark 47 depth bombs were dropped from 350 feet, the explosions straddling the U-boat abaft the conning tower. The U-boat slowed immediately and left a heavy oil slick in its wake.

At 0629, a plane *VF-4* from *U.S.S. Guadalcanal* made a strafing run from the U-boat's starboard beam, and at 0630 plane *VT-22* delivered a rocket attack from dead ahead of the U-boat, firing eight rockets at close range. All A/A fire from the U-boat had ceased. It was estimated that four of the rockets were direct hits. At 0631, *VF-4* again strafed the U-boat. At 0634, after the U-boat had submerged, *VT-22* dropped depth bombs. The drop was very close and was followed by a large underwater disturbance, an enormous air bubble, and green slick.

Three hours later, the sole survivor and a corpse were taken aboard an escort vessel, and three torpedo air flasks were recovered. Additional debris, including cork, cloth, food, a canvas bag, a sofa pillow, a leather jacket, and human remains were observed floating in the oil at the scene.

The sole survivor of *U-68* was the late Hans Kastrup.(Author's Note: *U-68* was a veteran boat scoring 33 kills, 195,000 tons, during its operational career. In addition to Atlantic patrols, the *Type IXC* 1,100 ton U-boat operated in the Indian Ocean where it sank seven allied merchantmen. The boat's initial commanding officer, Kapitänleutnant Karl-Friedrich Merten of the 1926 Naval Term accounted for 27 sinkings. He was awarded the Knight's Cross with Oak Leaves for his achievements and was promoted to Korvettenkapitän in April 1941.[68]

The *U.S.S. Guadalcanal (CVE-60)* escort carrier group, commanded by Captain Daniel V. Gallrey, Jr., USN, gained fame for its capture of the *U-505* in June of 1944. The U-boat currently resides on display at the Museum of Science and Industry in Chicago, Illinois.)[69]

U-378 in North Atlantic after being strafed by aircraft from USS CORE (CVE-13) - (U.S. National Archives)

U-378 (Germany)

Report of Antisubmarine Action by Aircraft/VC 13/U.S.S. Core (CVE-13)/October 20, 1943

The attacking section of one *TBF-1c* (Torpedo Bomber), pilot Lt. (jg) R.W. Hayman, USNR, and one *F4F-4* (Fighter), pilot Lt. Cmdr. C.W. Brewer, USN, was flying the second leg of an offensive search into an area reported by COMINCH (Commander in Chief, United States Fleet) to contain a refueling concentration. Overcast averaged 0.5, with scattered showers, though the area immediately over the scene of attack was clear. Visibility averaged 10 miles except in rain squalls. Sea was very rough, with a wind of 32 knots. The section had previously been flying on course 000 degrees at 6,000 feet searching visually, but had reduced to 4,000 feet to go under a cloud. Emerging from under the cloud, the submarine was sighted by the TBF pilot approximately 30 degrees off his starboard now, distance 3 miles. Submarine was black, fully surfaced, on course 330 degrees headed directly into the wind, and was making very little more than steerage way.

The *F4F* was flying close aboard and immediately caught the TBF pilot's hand signal, located the submarine, and started a strafing run, attacking the submarine from the port quarter, 30 degrees from astern. Sun on the port quarter made this run almost directly out of the sun. Fire was opened at 1,000 yards and tracers were seen by accompanying *TBF*'s crew to ricochet from the deck and conning tower. Approximately 1,000 rounds of ammunition were expended. Fire was concentrated on conning tower as the after guns appeared not to be manned. When *F4F* was at 500 feet a violent red flame was seen to break out, which completely filled the conning tower and extended aft to the upper gun platform. No antiaircraft fire was experienced. Pulling out of the strafing run, *F4F* turned left and gained a position which afforded unobstructed visibility of the depth charge attack.

The *TBF* had meanwhile turned right to lose altitude and gain a more favorable position for attack, the angle of direct attack being too steep. Attack was made from almost directly astern in a final glide of approximately 10 degrees. The pilot expended 40 to 50 rounds from each gun in strafing during approach. Bombs were released from 175 feet altitude, course 330 degrees, speed 240 knots. Bombs entered the water 100 feet and 170 feet over and slightly to the left of submarine's course, probably due to the plane being in a left skid at the time. The tip of the submarine's bow was obscured by the water thrown up by the explosion.

The submarine proceeded on into the depth charge disturbance. Some 30 seconds following the depth charge explosion, the submarine suddenly rolled over 60 degrees to port. Very shortly thereafter the bow and conning tower disappeared, leaving the stern above the surface at an angle of 30 degrees. Twenty to forty feet of stern was visible for 20 to 30 seconds, the length visible being varied by the waves. The stern then slowly disappeared. During this time the TBF made a turn to the left to gain position for an attack with a Mark 24 mine, taking pictures meanwhile.

Thirty seconds after the stern disappeared, the TBF made another run upwind along the course of the submarine, dropping a Mark 24 mine at the center of the disturbance left by the disappearing stern. The mine entered the water, ran straight ahead true and then made a sharp turn to the right. Approximately two minutes thereafter, the pilot and radioman observed a shock wave and a white flash (''as if someone had turned on a flashlight underwater'') 300 to 400 feet forward and to starboard of the point of the mine's entrance. This shock wave developed into a symmetrically round area of green water and air bubbles (as opposed to the disturbances left by breaking rollers). This symmetrical area faded out within a minute or two in the heavy seas.

No further evidence was observed by the plane, which remained on station for 2 hours and 15 minutes and kept the position marked with dye markers and smoke floats. Sea was so rough that dye markers which normally persist for a matter of hours were nearly obscured in 15 minutes.

The *USS Core* maintained a 24-hour guard on the two high frequencies of the area, and in addition two high frequencies of the adjacent area as defined in CSP 1774(A). Further, from one hour prior to darkness until daylight the *USS Core* guarded frequencies 385, 396, 437, and 490 kilocycles, and searched continuously from 200 to 650 kilocycles. Concurrently the three destroyers searched continuously as follows: *USS Greene* 200-350 kilocycles; *USS Belknap* 350-500 kilocycles; *USS Goldsborough* 500-650 kilocycles. No transmissions which might possibly have emanated from the attacked submarine were intercepted.

(Author's Note: Although *U-378* was launched in September 1941, it had only one sinking to its credit before it was sunk. On October 8, 1943 it attacked the Polish destroyer *Orkand* which was part of the escort group for Convoy SC.143. A single torpedo exploded in the ship's after magazine sinking the vessel in a matter of minutes. Lost with the ship was Commander Stanislaw Hryniewiecki, senior officer of all Polish destroyers.[70]

The sole survivor of *U-378* was Obersteuermann Karl-Heinz Brunkhorst. Records held at the U-Boot Archiv in Cuxhaven, Germany indicate that Brunkhorst went down with the ship that saved him.)

U-413 sole survivor Karl Hutterer - (U-Boot Archiv)

U-413 (Germany)

N.I.D. Interrogation of Sole Survivor of U-413, April 1945[71]

U-413, a 500-ton *Type VIIC* U-boat, belonging to the First Flotilla and based at Brest, France, was sunk at about 1000 on 20 August, 1944 by the destroyers *HMS Forester, HMS Vidette,* and *HMS Wensleydale,* jointly while on antisubmarine patrol in approximate position 50.21 N / 00.01 W (English Channel).

The commanding officer was Oberleutnant zur See Sachse (believed to be Dietrich Sachse, of the 1939 Naval Term).

Only one member of the U-boat's crew survived, Officer Oberleutnant (Engineer) Karl Hutterer, who was very security minded and a confirmed Nazi. Hutterer, who is on the active list in the German Navy, had spent most of his time in U-boats, and had served in the Baltic, North Sea, Norway and the Atlantic. Before joining *U-413* in February 1944, he had served on board *U-762* which ran on a reef off Norway and was then sent back to Memel.

U-413 sailed from Brest on 2 August 1944 to operate against shipping on the Allied convoy route between Southern England and the Baie de la Seine, after which she was to proceed to Norway.

At about 0900 on 20 August, there were indications that *U-413* was being pursued. She proceeded on her motors, at about 30 meters depth. The first series of depth charges fell wide of their target, but the second series was accurate, and water entered the U-boat aft and in the control room. Those of the crew who were in the control room immediately rushed to the bow compartment and closed the water-tight door behind them. The U-boat sank out of control and bottomed. The lights went out and the crew were soon up to their waists in water.

The Engineering Officer opened the forward hatch, through which he escaped. He did not know what happened to the rest of the crew.

(N.I.D. Note: At 0807 on 20 August, an ASDIC (Antisubmarine Detection Investigation Committee Apparatus) contact was obtained by *HMS Forester*, while on antisubmarine patrol with *HMS Wensleydale* and *HMS Vidette*. At 0915, *Forester* attacked with depth charges set to 150 feet, without result. *Vidette*, being the only ship present at that time with any salvos of bombs remaining, was then ordered to close and carry out a hedgehog attack, and at 0934 she attacked, the bombs being observed to fall on the centre bearing of the target from *Wensleydale*.[72] Bubbles and diesel oil came to the surface and one survivor was picked up by the *Wensleydale*. At 0952 *Wensleydale* made another depth charge attack, which was considered to have finished off the U-boat and left the area. Doubt was then expressed by *Forester* as to whether the U-boat was completely destroyed, as only a small amount of wreckage had come to the surface, which it was thought might have been fired from the torpedo tubes, as a ruse. After a further attack by *Forester*, with the same results, the position was left.

Wensleydale reported at 1325 that she had one uninjured prisoner on board and that the U-boat sunk was *U-413*, of the First Flotilla.)

U-413 realized limited success during its operational career. Launched in January 1942 at Danziger Werft, the boat's first commander, Kapitänleutnant Gustav Poel, winner of the Knight's Cross, included among his victories the sinking of the 1,100-ton British destroyer *HMS Warick (D-25)* in April of 1943. Other than the *Warick, U-413* was credited with only four successful merchantship attacks while under the command of Poel and later Sachse.[73]

U-419 sole survivor Dieter Giersberg - (U-Boot Archiv)

U-419 (Germany)

U-BOOT-ARCHIV

Laying of Keel:	November 7, 1941	Type:	VII C
Completion:	August 22, 1942		
Placed in Svc.:	November 18, 1942		
Built at:	Danzig Wharf		

Destiny of the Ship:

Sunk in the North Atlantic on October 8, 1943 by *Liberators* of the RAF Sq.86 and 120 and *Sunderland* of the RCAF Sq.423.

48 dead—captain was the only one who was rescued

Position of Sinking: 56°31′N 27°05′W Field P.O. No. M-51 062

Part of the following flotillas:

8th U-Flotilla from November 1942 to July 1943

11th U-Flotilla from August 1943 to October 1943

Captains:

Ltjg Dietrich GIERSBERG November 1942 to October 1943

Patrol Officers:

Ens. Franz HEIMEL + (deceased)
Ens.Reserve Nicolaus THEIS +

Commanding Engineer:

Lt. Eng. Wolfgang CORNELIUS +

Machinist Albrecht BRAND +
Machinist Hellmut GRUNERT +

Doctor on Board:

Medic Josef LEIDINGER +

Piloting Chief:

Chief Petty Officer Max ADOMEIT +

Sole Undertaking:

Left Bergen September 13, 1943

September 27	in the mid North Atlantic with the Group "Roabach" engaged at Convoy ON. 203
October 6	with Group "Roabach" against Convoy SC. 143 and HX. 259
October 8	sinking of the ship Report of the captain as sole survivor in the publications regarding the ship
Tower Marking:	Shield with two crossed swords

Report of the Captain, Lt.jg Dietrich Giersberg:

"On September 13, 1943, U-419 left Bergen with the task to operate in the North Atlantic against enemy convoys. The position in the Atlantic as prescribed was reached and the waiting there occurred without noteworthy events, except for constant storms. In the afternoon of October 7th, a ship of the group reported enemy destroyers. Since this raised the assumption that a convoy was in the area, we directed our operations towards them. During the night of October 8th, U-419 made contact with two destroyers but was shaken off by them. Approximately an hour later a detonation could be observed ahead of the ship, accompanied by heavy firing from the air. In the morning hours two destroyers were sighted in the other direction and shortly after that, a *Liberator* flew over U-419 without its being noticed. After another hour smoke was noticed from the steering board, and a convoy was expected. At the same time the attack of a four-engine plane on a U-boat which was getting ready for the dive could be observed. Since we had to be noticed by the airplane shortly, we dived down for about 20 minutes. Ten minutes after resurfacing, U-419 was attacked by a *Liberator*. Since a successful diving to safe depth was uncertain and meant the loss of sight of the convoy, 'FT' sighting report was going to be made, and the attacking plane was put under fire with the defense weapons. A disturbance at the side regulator of the 'Vierling' [quarter] occurred at the decisive moment (most probably caused by high sea, but not yet apparent when shot at) and the missing of a 2-cm in 'single lafettes' enabled the plane to throw down its bombs without interference. Both (about 2,000 kg-bombs) hit the water approximately 10m away from the boat. Shortly thereafter there was a huge detonation which lifted the whole ship (I broke my left leg during this) and within seconds the ship shot down into the depth, assumably caused by the tearing up of the diving cells and the running engines.

"After having gotten rid of my leather gear, I reached the surface after about two minutes and was swimming, and I saw not one person of the crew, and I also did not sight anybody to the point when I got fished out by an English destroyer (assumably

Orilli), so that I must assume that they all were thrown down into the depth.

signed/Dietrich Giersberg''

U-1199 (Germany)

N.I.D. Interrogation of Sole Survivor of U-1199, April 1945[74]

U-1199, a 500-ton *Type VIIC* boat, operating from Bergen, Norway and probably belonging to the Eleventh Flotilla, was sunk at 1620 on 21 January, 1945 by *HMS Icarus* in position 074 degrees, Wolf Rock 4 miles, having been previously attacked and seriously damaged by *HMS Mignonette*. The commanding officer was Kapitänleutnant Rolf Nollmann.

U-1199 sailed from Bergen on 31 December, 1944, unaccompanied, carrying provisions for about 9 weeks. The U-boat proceeded through the Rosengarten and off the west coast of Ireland, the last position noted by the sole survivor, Obersteuermann Friedrich Claussen (Navigator) being somewhere to the southwest of the Scillies as they were approaching the Channel from the Atlantic.

The prisoner declared that he had never been allowed to plot their course on the chart, but took his orders from the commanding officer, who himself acted as navigator and gave him bearings by observing lights at periscope depth. He remembered that the commanding officer had sighted the Wolf Rock lighthouse from a distance of 5 miles, half an hour before the engagement.

On the 21st of January a convoy was heard and the U-boat came to periscope depth. The commanding officer sighted about 60 ships and a spread of torpedoes was fired. The prisoner believed that they hit one 10,000-ton and one 8,000-ton ship.

(N.I.D. Note: *SS George Hawley* in convoy TBC.45 was torpedoed in position 180 degrees Longships 4 miles at 1448/21st January. Ship was holed in the engine room and taken in tow by the tug *Allegiance*. Both ships arrived in Falmouth at 0530 on the 22nd. The *Hawley* was a total loss.)

The U-boat bottomed and shortly afterwards experienced the effects of the first depth charge attack, which caused a small leak in the bow compartment, which subsequently became a large inrush of water; the main motors were put out of action. The attack continued for several hours, successive patterns of depth charges causing still further damage; the magnetic compass was smashed, and the rotary converters dislodged. The after control room bulkhead was closed and the prisoner was ignorant of what happened aft. In the forward compartment the water was rising rapidly, and when it had risen 3 feet above the floorplates, the commanding officer ordered the crew to don their life jackets. The prisoner said that he put the mouthpiece of his escape lung into his mouth and ascribes the loss of the rest of the crew to the fact that they failed to do this and were suffocated by chlorine gas, which was forming by this time. He saw men collapsing one by one.

(N.I.D. Note: At 1320/21st January, 1945, *HMS Mignonette*, escorting Convoy HXA.331, closed to 300 yards on the starboard side of the *George Hawley* and commenced "Observant," dropping single depth charges.[75] At 1335 a contact was gained at 600 yards and immediately attacked with depth charges.

At 1416 a hedgehog attack was made on a stationary target in the vicinity of the first contact, followed by a second depth charge attack. A second hedgehog attack was made at 1447 and about 20 minutes later contact was re-established and depth charged. Contact was then turned over to *HMS Icarus*.)

A final pattern of depth charges tore a hole in the wardroom of the U-boat and the forward part of the boat began to fill even more rapidly with water. The commanding officer ordered the prisoner to open the conning tower hatch which, although stiff at first, suddenly flew open and the prisoner was blown up through it into the water. There was no time to help any of the others who were in the conning tower.

(N.I.D. Note: *HMS Icarus* obtained contact at 1618/22nd January, 1945 and carried out one hedgehog and two depth charge attacks. Wood wreckage, oil, and large bubbles were observed and when turning for the third attack a survivor was picked up. The U-boat was believed to have been sunk at 1620A/21st in position 074 degrees Wolf Rock 4 miles.)

The prisoner stated that all the high pressure air bottles were full at the time of the sinking and he believed that the after part of the boat was not flooded, in which case it would be possible to raise *U-1199* without much difficulty.

No attempt was made to refloat the U-boat.

I-365 (Japan)

U.S.S. SCABBARDFISH(SS397)-Report of Second War Patrol (Partial)[76]

27 November 1944

0500 On new lifeguard station.

1455 Five contacts on SD radar answering IFF (Identification Friend or Foe). *B-29*s homeward bound from 2nd Tokyo raid. Saw four through clouds.

28 November 1944

0500 Patrolling trade routes between TOKYO and BONIN ISLAND. Wind and sea increasing.

0603 Dove to charge eight remaining torpedoes and ride out storm as well.

1647 Surfaced. Headed for lifeguard station.

29 November 1944

0500 Patrolling near lifeguard station.

0615 Sighted ship bearing 009 degrees True, distance about 15,000 yards through high periscope. Commenced ending around through Westward.

0844 On target's track up ahead range about 18,000 yards. We had just about decided to dive and head towards target now identified as a submarine when lookout reported an enemy plane distance about fifteen miles closing. Dived and reversed course heading for target. Sea swells from 6 to 10 feet and holding depth at 60 feet troublesome.

0918 About worked myself into believing enemy plane had warned submarine and that he had submerged, when JP came through with a 357° bearing.

0921 First periscope look for bearing. Swells too high and was worried about my scope being sighted. Target has slightly bulbous bow. Subsequent looks showed a gun forward and an indistinct numeral resembling 133 in white letters painted on the forward port curve of his black bridge structure. Target zigzagging on base course 270 degrees, speed 11 knots. Decided on bow tube shot if possible since we have six torpedoes forward and only two aft; but a zig toward us gave a sharp bow angle at 3,000 yards forcing a stern tube shot. With 120 port track, gyro angle about 153 degrees generated range 1500 yards.

0935 Fired #7 torpedo.

0935 Fired #10 torpedo. Ranges were poor. Should have hit at about 1-39 for second torpedo for 1625 yards run, but 1 minute and 59 seconds after firing second torpedo, heard a delightful explosion rewarding our efforts.

0937 Observed torpedo hit followed by brownish white smoke.

0939 Two loud explosions. Soundman put breaking up noises on loud speaker for benefit of conning tower personnel. Prepared to surface.

0948 Heard one long drawn out shrill screech like bleeding down high pressure air bottle followed by one terrific explosion and much rain. That must have been the air bottles and hull collapsing at deep submergence. Made a thorough search through scope, neither plane nor target in sight.

0950 Surfaced. Headed for last true bearing of target for possible survivors.

0953 Entered huge oil slick covered with floating pieces of wooden decking.

0954 Sighted five heads bobbing up and down. Commenced picking up survivors. All but one refused to come aboard. Only one man, whom we believe to be a torpedoman, swam alongside and took the line offered him. He was pretty far gone from the cold water, injury and shock but Byork, PhM1c, did a splendid job of reviving him and taping up a busted rib. At present time, he is very happy about his decision to come aboard. Refused volunteers who offered to swim to survivors and force them to come aboard because of heavy sea, thick scum of poor grade diesel oil, and possible presence of escort aircraft in vicinity. Stood by until satisfied all survivors in water had perished then pulled clear of area. Took several pictures of prisoner coming aboard. One run, one hit, no errors, 49 Nips left aboard. Prisoner stated submarine was *I-365* and that she had been on a 50 day patrol to Guam.

1159 Sent report of results to ComSubPac.

(Author's Note: *I-365* was sunk by *Scabbardfish* at position 34.44N / 141.01E. Twelve days earlier she sent the Japanese cargo ship *Kisarayi Maru* to the bottom 600 miles east of Kyushu.[77] *I-365* was commanded by Lieutenant Commander Motoh Nakamura. The identification of the sole survivor is unknown.)[78]

I-373 (Japan)

U.S.S. SPIKEFISH(SS404)-Report of Fourth War Patrol (Partial)[79]

13 August 1945

0440(H) Dived.

1107(H) Surfaced.

1200(H) Position: Lat. 29.20N Long. 124.01E.

2010(H) SJ radar contact bearing 032(T), range 9800 yards. S/C #11. Position: Lat. 29.32N Long. 124.56E. Had strong signal on APR at 145 M.C. at this time, pulse rate 500, pulse width 8-10.

2018(H) Upon closing bearing to attempt identification, sighted large submarine at range 3500 yards. APR signal was now at saturation. Commenced opening range rapidly and stationed tracking party. It was a dark night, with moon at first quarter, but target may have seen us or made radar contact.

2041(H) Target tracking on base course 230(T), speed 10, zigging frequently. Sent contact report.

2118(H) Following a sudden zig of target to course 130(T), we lost SJ contact and APR signal at almost the same time. Target was bearing 032(T), range 9500 yards when we lost him.

2122(H) Stopped, rigged out sound heads, and listened. Target had dived, but I hoped to be on hand when he surfaced.

2148(H) Commenced a radar and sound search on easterly and westerly courses, keeping far enough from target's diving point to prevent his closing us submerged. The moon was now down.

2151(H) Received message from ComSubPac advising us that contact was probably enemy.

2313(H) Target had now been down two hours unless he had surfaced and gotten away. Decided to open out from the target's track to the northwestward for an hour, then steer the reverse of his base course on a track parallel to his. I based this decision on a hunch that his last zig to 130 may have been a feint, and that he probably reversed course again after he dived. The existence of a restricted area to the eastward also made this a likely possibility. Went ahead on three engines on course 315(T).

14 August 1945

0000(H) Came to course 045(T).

0007(H) SJ contact bearing 075(T), range 8600 yards. Same target, but he was not using his radar now. Commenced tracking from ahead, keeping the range at about 9000 yards. Same course and speed as before, zigging 25 to 30 degrees from base course every 2 or 3 minutes.

0115(H) Received message from ComSubPac stating that no friendly forces were known to be in the area. Although all indications were that the target was a Japanese submarine, I could not be positive without seeing him. For this reason, I decided upon a dawn submerged attack. It had to be right at daybreak, since I expected the target to dive again at dawn, and since the seas were glassy calm.

0402(H) Headed toward target and dived slightly to westward of his track. Range 13,400 yards. Sunrise at 0510.

0405(H) Sound picked up screws. Heard occasional pings on 14. 7 K.C., typically Japanese. Had excellent sound bearings throughout approach.

0412(H) ST range, 5400 yards.

0419(H) Target in sight, definitely a Jap, range 3000 yards. He was perfectly silhouetted, while my background was very dark.

0424(H) Commenced firing salvo of six torpedoes from bow tubes on 60 starboard track, torpedo run 1300 yards, average gyros 2 left, depth set at 20 feet.

0425-10(H) Timed hit for number 3 torpedo.

0425-20(H) Timed hit for number 4 torpedo. Saw target's bow projecting at a large angle from a pall of smoke and disappear. Heard loud sounds of escaping air.

0531(H) Surfaced and headed for point of attack at Lat. 29.02N Long. 123.53E.

0540(H) Passed through heavy accumulation of diesel oil, large quantities of debris, all resembling wooden decking, and a large assortment of dead fish. Saw five Japanese floating and playing dead. Couldn't interest any of them in coming aboard, even with one of our prisoners from the sea truck (sunk 11 August) trying to persuade them. Finally succeeded in looping a life line around the neck of one, pulled him over the fantail, and cleared the area. The prisoner was uninjured but covered with oil. He identified the target as I-382.

0806(H) Sighted *PBM* bearing 160(T), distance 15 miles. Talked to him on VHF.

0900(T) Sent *SPIKEFISH* sixth to ComSubPac.

0928(T) Dived for a little rest.

1200(H) Position: Lat. 29.30N Long. 124.38E.

1707(H) Surfaced and departed the area.

(Author's Note: Japanese submarine sunk was in fact *I-373* under the command of Lieutenant Commander Yukio Inoba. *I-373* was the last Japanese submarine destroyed in the war. The identification of the sole survivor is unknown.)[80]

EPILOGUE

For those interested in reading more about sole survivors of mishaps at sea there exists various international maritime museums and archives that can be contacted for such information.

The Maritime Information Center at the National Maritime Museum in Greenwich, England holds an extensive collection of books on shipwrecks and shipping disasters. The collection also includes the Board of Trade Wreck Registers from 1855 to 1898 and the museum's own wreck registers compiled by members of its staff. Among their published works are collected stories of various wrecks around the world.

The Peabody Museum founded in 1799 and located in Salem, Massachusetts holds over 300 volumes dealing with shipwrecks. From one reference, *Accounts of Shipwrecks* by a friend of Seaman, Joseph Griffin publisher, Brunswick, Maine 1823, the following sole survivors were extracted:

John Cornelius	1646	*Gallot Delft*

Alexander Selkirk	1704	*Cinq Portes*
Philip Ashton	1722	
-Purnell	1759	*Br. Tyrel*
-McDaniel	1759	*Ship Ann & Mary*
Mr. Schabeacq	1799	*Frigate LaLatine*
Robert Scotney	1802	*Br. Thomas*
one crewman	1806	*Ship Essex*
George Fracker	1817	*Ship Jane*
-Drew (female)	1820	*Nautilus*
Negro woman	1821	*Schooner Blake*
James Brock	1835	

Another source is the Calvert Marine Museum at Solomons, Maryland. Included in its extensive collection is the *Merchant Vessels of the United States* series which lists casualties to American vessels occurring from 1906 through 1942. These reports list the number of individuals on board the vessel involved in the casualty as well as the number of lives lost. As an example, in the 1911 edition 325 vessels were lost. Of this number there were six instances of sole survivors.

Unfortunately, personal accounts by sole survivors of distant decades were most often not recorded and one is left only with statistics and an exhaustive research task in order to find further documentation of the incidents.

The selection of incidents for this journal which centered around World War II made our endeavor much easier since relevant official documents could be found in U.S. and foreign national and military museums and archives. However, the task was not always easy since some countries seal their wartime records for as long as 75 years. Also, by selecting a war setting, sole survivor incidents proved to be more dramatic since those plying the sea routes of the world had to survive two equally dangerous elements, a stalking enemy and the unpredictable hazards of the sea.

APPENDIX

SOLE SURVIVORS OF THE SEA

1. British, Allied, and Neutral Merchant Vessels sunk or Destroyed by War Causes 1939-1945 Where a Lone Seaman Survived. (1)

Date	*Ship's Name*	*Ctry(2)*	*Location*	*Cause*	*Sole Survivor*
12/13/39	*William Hallet*	Br	Tyne Area	Mine	Unknown
01/27/40	*Ho Sanger*	No	58.25N/1.53W	Mine	Unknown
05/18/40	*Pia*	Du	Between Dunkirk & Gravelines	Mine	Unknown
06/06/40	*Francis Massey*	Br	55.33N/8.26W	*U-48*	Unknown
08/25/40	*Empire Merlin*	Br	58.30N/10.15W	*U-48*	Unknown
08/31/40	*Har Zion*	Br	56.20N/10W	*U-59*	Unknown
09/04/40	*Joseph Swan*	Br	52.50N/29E	E-Boat	Unknown
09/19/40	*Almirante Jose de Carranza*	Sp	16nm NW C. Villano	It sub. *Marconi*	Unknown
11/12/40	*Argus*	Br	199 degrees 3 cables from S. Oaze buoy	Mine	Archie Smith

02/17/41	*Gairsoppa*	Br	300nm SW Galway	*U-101*	Richard Ayres
03/01/41	*Pacific*	Br	180nm WSW Sydero	*U-95*	Unknown
03/02/41	*Augvald*	No	150nm NW Loch Ewe	*U-147*	Unknown
04/02/41	*Castlehill*	Br	10nm SE Mine Head	Aircraft	Unknown
04/03/41	*HMS Bah Ram*	Br	In North Channel	Under-water Explosion	Unknown
05/03/41	*Corbet*	Br	Herculaneum back entrance Liverpool	Aircraft	Unknown
05/08/41	*HMS Thistle*	Br	52.28N/1.47E	Mine	Unknown
02/22/42	*W.D. Anderson*	Br	27.9N/80.15W	*U-504*	Unknown
02/24/42	*Struma*	Pa	Off entrance to Bosporus	Explo-sion	Unknown
02/28/42	*Bayou*	Pa	300nm off Trinidad	*U-129*	Unknown
03/06/42	*Steel Age*	Am	600nm south Trinidad	*U-129*	Unknown
03/14/42	*Tolten*	Cl	40.10N/73.50W	*U-404*	Unknown
04/20/42	*Chenango*	Pa	36.25N/74.55W	*U-84*	Unknown
05/17/42	*San Victorio*	Br	11.40N/62.32W	*U-155*	A. Ryan
07/06/42	*Mamatu*	Br	0.11S/144.12E	(jp)*Ro-38*	Unknown
10/16/42	*W.C. Teagle*	Br	57N/25W	*U-558*	N.D. Houston
11/23/42	*Benlomond*	Br	00.30N/38.45W	*U-172*	Poon Lim
11/29/42	*Sawokla*	Am	23S/80.54E	Raider *Widder*	Unknown
12/07/42	*Ceramic*	Br	40.30N/40.20W	*U-515*	Eric Munday
12/07/42	*Henry Stanley*	Br	40.35N/39.40W	*U-103*	Richard Jones
12/21/42	*Queen City*	Br	00.49S/41.34W	It sub. *Tazzoli*	Unknown
02/15/43	*Atlantic Sun*	Am	33.34N/77.25W	*U-124*	William Golobich
03/09/43	*Puerto Rican*	Am	66.44N/10.41W	*U-586*	August Wallen-haupt
03/13/43	*Sembilangan*	Du	42.45N/13.50W	*U-107*	Unknown
03/28/43	*Roushdy*	Eg	31.46N/34.23E	*U-81*	Unknown
04/02/43	*Simon Duhamel II*	Fr	36.1N/2.29W	*U-755*	Unknown

04/17/43	*Sembilan*	Du	31.30S/33.30E	(It) *DaVinci*	Unknown
05/11/44	*Empire Heath*	Br	19S/31W	*U-129*	Unknown
12/29/44	*Venersborg*	Sw	200nm SW of Utklippan	Explosion	Unknown
01/12/45	*Treern*	No	39.6N/23.14E	Mine	Unknown
01/13/45	*Beltana*	Sw	SW of Paternoster	Mine	Unknown
01/21/45	*Ga Latea*	No	53.40N/5.23W	Mine	Unknown

2. Others: (3)

10/20/16	*James B. Colgate*	Am	Lake Erie	Storm	Walter Grashaw
06/08/40	*HMS Acasta*	Br	Norwegian Sea	*Scharnhorst/ Gneisenau*	G. Carter
08/01/40	*HMS Spearfish* (sub)	Br	Capenose Head	*U-34*	Able Seaman William V. Pester
10/18/40	*HMS H. 49* (sub)	Br	Off Dutch Coast	*Trawlers*	Lead Stocker George W. Oliver
12/06/41	*HMS Perseus* (sub)	Br	Off western coast of Greece	Mine	John H. Capes
12/19/41	*HMS Neptune (4)*	Br	20nm off Tripoli Harbor	Mine	John N. Walton
10/02/42	*U-512*	Gr	50nm North of Cayenne	*99th US Bomb Sqd*	Francissk Machon
03/03/43	*Doggerbank*	Gr	1000nm North of Canaries	*U-43*	Fritz Kuert
04/15/43	*Archimede* (sub)	It	3.23S/30.38W	USN *VP-83*	Giuseppe Lococo
06/02/43	*U-521*	Gr	Off Delaware Capes	USN *PC-565*	Klaus Bargsten
10/08/43	*U-419*	Gr	51.36N/27.05W	Br *Sqd 86*	Dietrich Giersberg
10/16/43	*U-533*	Gr	Gulf of Oman	RAF *Sqd 244*	Gunther Schmidt
10/20/43	*U-378*	Gr	47.40N/28.27W	USN *VC-13*	Karl Heinz Brunkhorst

03/26/44	*Tullibee(SS284)*	Am	NW Palau Isle	Jp Destroyer	Clifford W. Kuykendall
04/10/44	*U-68*	Gr	33.25N/18.59W	USN *VC-58*	Hans Kastrup
06/14/44	*HMS Sickle* (sub)	Br	Aegean Sea	Mine	Able Seamen Richard Blake
08/20/44	*U-413*	Gr	50.21N/00.01W	HMS *Forester/ Vidette/ Wensley-dale*	Karl Hutterer
11/29/44	*I-365*	Jp	34.44N/141.01E	*USS Scabbardfish (SS397)*	Unknown
01/21/45	*U-1199*	Gr	49.57N/05.42W	*HMS Icarus/ Mignon-ette*	Friedrich Claussen
02/17/45	*HMS Bluebell*	Br	Off Kola Inlet	*U-711*	A.E.G. Holmes
02/17/45	*U-425*	Gr	69.39N/33.50W	*HMS Lark/ Alnwick Castle*	H. Lochner
04/01/45	*Awa Maru*	Jp	Taiwan Strait	*USS Queenfish (SS393)*	Kantaro Shimoda
04/15/45	*U-103*	Gr	Gdynia	Allied Bombers	Adolf Janssen
04/23/45	*U-183*	Gr	04.56S/112.52E	*USS Besugo (SS321)*	Karl Wisniewski
08/14/45	*I-373*	Jp	29.02N/123.53E	*USS Spikefish (SS404)*	Unknown
03/22/73	*Norse Variant*	No	36.53N/70.31W	Storm	Stein Gabrielsen
04/11/93	*Moby Prince*	It	3nm off Leghorn	Collision	Alessio Bertrand

Notes:

(1) Lloyd's War Losses, The Second World War, 3 September 1939-14 August 1945, Vol 1.

(2) Am-American, Br-British, Cl-Chilean, Du-Dutch, Gr-Greek, It-Italian, Jp-Japanese, No-Norwegian, Pa-Panamanian, Sp-Spanish, Sw-Swedish.

(3) World War II warships and recent incidents not listed in Lloyd's.

(4) At the time of its last action, *HMS Neptune* was in the process of being transferred to the New Zealand Navy. Of the 765 men lost, 150 were New Zealanders.

NOTES TO TEXT

1. The primary reference source used to recount the Richard Ayres story was *In Peril on the Sea* by David Masters, pp. 11-24.
2. Rohwer, *Axis Submarine Successes 1939-1945*, p. 43.
3. *London Gazette-1941*, pp. 1143-1144.
4. Mrs. Richard Ayres, correspondence, 15 May 1993.
5. The primary reference source for this remarkable incidence of sole survival is the book, *Sole Survivor*, by Ruthanne Lum McCunn. Ms. McCunn based her work on interviews with Poon Lim, his wife, and relatives, American and British intelligence reports, and The Ben Line histories. In addition, this author was able to elicit further information regarding the Poon Lim story through personal correspondence with Ms. McCunn in June 1993. Other sources used were an article titled, ''They Survived the Sea'' written by Lt. Comdr. Samuel F. Harby, USNR and published in the May 1945 issue of *The National Geographic* magazine (pp. 637-640), and National Archives and Records Administration (hereinafter NARA) Modern Military Branch, Military

Archives Division, Records Group (hereinafter RG) 38: *German Naval Records World War II: Kreigstagebücher (German War Diary, hereafter KTB), U-123,* 23 November 1942.
6. Matthews, *The Guinness Book of Records 1993,* p. 195.
7. Two main reference sources were used to relate the unique sole survivor story of Fritz Kuert, e.g., *The Ship With Five Names,* by Charles Gibson and U.S. Intelligence debriefs of Mr. Kuert in Aruba (Lesser Antilles), and the Office of Naval Intelligence in Washington, D.C./NARA RG 38: *Reports of Interrogations and Documents 1941-45.*
8. Roskill, *The War at Sea 1939-1945 vol. 1,* p. 381.
9. More than 40 whalebacks, both steamers and barges, were built between 1888 and 1898, and for a time it was thought that the whaleback principle would revolutionize the shipping world.

A long, narrow hull with a flat bottom but rounded sides that tapered very nearly to a point fore and aft, the whaleback resembled a floating cigar. The taper was carried upward from the keel so that the sides and bottom converged with the deck above the water line (like a snout).

The theory behind the construction was that a hull with rounded sides and decks and a spoon-shaped bow would offer minimal resistance to wind and wave. Rather than fight against the elements as straight vessels do, the whaleback could run with the decks awash. Lydecker, *Pigboat,* Summation by researcher for The Great Lakes Historical Society.
10. The primary source of information used to recount Captain Grashaw's sole survivor experience was The Great Lakes Historical Society which holds numerous documents on the incident.
11. Nelson B. Grashaw, correspondence, 7 May 1991.
12. Wheal, Pope & Taylor, *Encyclopedia of The Second World War,* pp. 343-344.
13. Roscoe, *United States Destroyer Operations in World War II,* pp. 470-471.
14. Potter, *Sea Power,* pp. 349-350.
15. Rohwer, *Axis Submarine Successes 1939-1945,* pp. 274-275.
16. *Action Report, USS Morrison (DD560), 5 April 1945.*
17. Hashimoto, *Sunk,* pp. 151-152.

18. Most of the material used in this writing of sole survivor Captain Richard Jones came from a relative of the captain, Mr. Emrys Jones. Mr. Jones provided invaluable detail regarding Captain Jones' early seagoing years and the final journey of the *Henry Stanley*. Mr. Jones additionally allowed us to use the fine photograph of Captain Jones to illustrate the story. Also used: NARA, *KTB U-103*, 6, 7 December 1942.
19. Rohwer, *Axis Submarine Successes 1939-1945*, pp. 66-67.
20. The primary reference source for this account was: *ADM 199, Vols. 2130-2148: U.K. Shipping Casualties Section/Trade Division: Report of an interview with Sapper E. Munday, Royal Engineers, 14 August 1945.*
21. NARA, *KTB U-515*, 6-7 December 1942.
22. Morison, *History of United States Naval Operations in World War II, The Atlantic Battle Won, May 1943-May 1945, vol. X*, p. 282.
23. Mason, *The Atlantic War Remembered*, pp. 125-127.
24. Wheal, Pope, Taylor, *Encyclopedia of the Second World War*, p. 528.
25. Roskill, *The War at Sea, vol. III, Part II*, pp. 256-257.
26. *Ships of the ESSO Fleet in World War II*, p. 331.
27. *Commanding Officer, HMS Zest: Sinking of HMS Bluebell, 26th February 1945.*
28. Morison, *History of United States Naval Operations in World War II, The Atlantic Battle Won May 1939-May 1945, vol. X*, p. 312.
29. Ibid. pp. 312-313.
30. Thomas Cooper & Co., 71 St. Mary Avenue, London E.C. 3, *W.C. Teagle* Statutory Declaration of Norman Douglas Houston, First Wireless Officer on *W.C. Teagle*, December 30, 1941 pm.
31. Vat, *The Atlantic Campaign*, p. 210.
32. *Ships of the ESSO Fleet in World War II*, pp. 71-73.
33. Rohwer, *Axis Submarine Successes 1939-1945*, p. 69.
34. Morison, *History of U.S. Naval Operations in World War II, Battle of the Atlantic, vol. 1, September 1939-May 1943*, p. 93.
35. Rohwer, *Axis Submarine Successes 1939-1945*, pp. 40-73.
36. Primary reference sources used in this account include: (1) Operational Archives, U.S. Naval Historical Center (hereafter

OA/NHC): *XXXVI Fighter Command, AirTask Force, Report of November 1, 1942. Subject: Sinking of Submarine,* (2) *NARA: RG 38: Reports of Interrogations and Documents 1941-1945,* (3) OA/NHC: *U.S.S. Ellis DD-154: Daily War Diary, Monday 12 October 1942,* (4) Morison, *History of United States Naval Operations in World War II, The Battle of the Atlantic, vol. 1, September 1939-May 1943,* p. 350, and (5) Krammer, *Nazi Prisoners of War in America,* p. 180.
37. Rohwer, *Axis Submarine Successes 1939-1945,* pp. 92-99.
38. Maritime Royal Artillery Old Comrades Association, correspondence, 1st March 1993.
39. The primary reference source for this account was: *ADM 199, Vols. 2130-2148: U.K. Shipping Casualties Section/Trade Division: Report of an interview with a maritime D.E.M.S. Gunner, Mr. A. Ryan, 30th November, 1942.* (D.E.M.S.-Defensively Equipped Merchant Ships)
40. *U.S. Submarine Losses-World War II,* p. 174.
41. References used for relating the story of sole survivor Nostromo Giuseppe Lococo included: NARA: *U.S. Navy Department, Office of the Chief of Naval Operations, Washington, O.N.I. (Office of Naval Intelligence) 250-I/Serial 1: Report on the Interrogation of Presumably Sole Survivor from Archimede sunk 15 April 1943. Signed Lt. Ducibella, 2 July 1943;* OA/NHC: *Action Report, Commander Patrol Squadron 83, Serial 024, 18 April 1943: Antisubmarine Action Report Covering Attack on 15 April 1943 in Lat. 03.23S, Long. 30.38W by PBY-5A which crippled a surfaced submarine and led to its destruction;* and correspondence with Amm. Div. Sicurezza, Ufficio Storica della Marina Militare, Rome, Italy, 26 April 1993.
42. Primary source used for this sole survivor account was OA/NHC: *U.S. Navy Department, Office of the Chief of Naval Operations, Washington, O.N.I. (Office of Naval Intelligence) 250-G/Serial 14: Report on the Interrogation of Sole Survivor from U-521 sunk on 2 June 1943.*
43. Rohwer, *Axis Submarine Successes 1939-1945,* pp. 132, 133, 136, 137, 149, 152, 159, 303.
44. Morison, *History of United States Naval Operations in World War II, The Atlantic Battle Won, May 1943-May 1945, vol. X,* pp. 181-182.

45. The primary reference source used to tell the sole survival story of Leading Seaman J. Walton was Smith & Walker, *Sea Battles in Close-Up: The Battle of the Malta Striking Forces*, pp. 95-103.
46. Paravanes-Large torpedo shaped devices towed under water on either side of ships and equipped with sharp teeth for cutting moorings of submerged mines allowing them to float and be destroyed.
47. Correspondence with John Norman Walton, 6 December 1993.
48. Edward Gallagher, Correspondence with, 14 September 1993.
49. The primary reference source used to relate the survival of John H. Capes of *HMS Perseus* was *HMS Medway 11-Recommendation for Decoration or Mention in Dispatches in the Case of John H. Capes, 14th July 1943*. Also, Evans, A.S., *Beneath The Waves*, pp. XX
50. *U.S. Submarine Losses-World War II*, backside of title page.
51. Ibid. p. 1.
52. OA/NHC: *Submarines Pacific: POW Statements/U.S.S. Tullibee (SS-284)-Statement of Kuykendall, Clifford Weldon, GM2/c, 356-73-89*, pp. 1-5.
53. Roskill, *The War at Sea 1939-1945, vol. 1*, pp. 194-195.
54. Wheal, Pope, & Taylor, *Encyclopedia of the Second World War*, p. 114.
55. Roskill, *The War at Sea 1939-1945, vol. 1*, pp. 194-195.
56. Churchill, *Memoirs of the Second World War*, pp. 217-218.
57. Primary reference sources used in this sole survivor account included: Giese/Wise, "Hitler's U-Boats in the Pacific," *Sea Classics*, June 1991, pp. 12-17, 64-66; Saville, "German Submarines in the Far East," U.S. Naval Institute *Proceedings*, August 1961, pp. 80-92; Rumpf, *Bootsmann Gunther Schmidt: Sole Survivor of U-533*, research paper.
58. Reference sources used in the sole survivor story of Warrant Officer Karl Wisniewski were: *U-Boot Archiv (Cuxhaven) Report, "Ein Mann Uberlebt die Katastrophe von U-183" (One Man Survives the Catastrophy of U-183)*; NARA: *Seventh Fleet Intelligence Center: Interrogation of prisoner taken from German Submarine U-183, sunk by*

U.S.S. Besugo on 23 April 1945; U.S.S. Besugo (SS321), Report of Fourth Patrol.
59. *KTB U-106,* 23 October 1941.
60. Reference sources used in this account included: Molstad-Andresen, "Only One Came Back," *The Reader's Digest, March 1976, pp. 64-68;* Montgomery, "Shipwrecked Sailor Saved After 3 Days," *The New York Times, March 26, 1973,* p. 1 col. 2.; "CGd Pilot, AF Aircraft Navy Carrier in Rescue," *Navy Times, April 25, 1973,* p. 8.
61. Reference sources used in the "Livorno Disaster" include: Gower, "Ferry Survivor Re-Lives Horror," *World Report, April 12, 1991,* p. 7; Pedrick, "Italian Ferry, Oil Tanker Collide; 138 Feared Dead," *The Washington Post, April 12, 1991.*
62. *U.S. Submarine Losses-World War II,* p. 164.
63. Rohwer, *Axis Submarine Successes 1939-1945,* pp. 111, 113, 128, 149, 166, 167.
64. *U.S. Submarine Losses-World War II,* p. 164.
65. *U.S. Submarine Losses-World War II,* p. 164.
66. Rohwer, *Axis Submarine Successes 1939-1945,* pp. 77, 198, 201, 202. *U.S. Submarine Losses-World War II,* p. 169.
67. NARA RG 38 Box 1: *U.S. Navy Department, Office of the Chief of Naval Operations, Washington, O.N.I. (Office of Naval Intelligence) Report of Interrogation: U-68.*
68. Rohwer, *Axis Submarine Successes 1939-1945,* pp. 60, 66, 70, 71, 82, 83, 85, 86, 88, 101, 102, 104, 105, 122, 123, 157, 173, 174, 264, 265, 310.
69. Museum of Science and Industry, Chicago, Illinois, (brochure) *The Story of the U-505,* pp. 1-33.
70. Morison, *History of United States Naval Operations in World War II, The Atlantic Battle Won, May 1943-May 1945, vol. X,* pp. 147-148, 161.
71. OA/NHC: *N.I.D. (Naval Intelligence Division) Report of: Interrogation of Sole Survivor of U-413, April 1945.*
72. Hedgehog—An "ahead-thrown" antisubmarine weapon consisting of a steel cradle which housed 24 explosive projectiles. Once fired out into the sea, the projectiles would sink swiftly and explode upon contact with a target.

73. Rohwer, *Axis Submarine Successes 1939-1945*, pp. 136, 147, 148, 178, 184, 312.
74. OA/NHC: *N.I.D. (Naval Intelligence Division) Report of Interrogation of Sole Survivor of U-1199, April 1945.*
75. "Observant"—Anti-submarine tactical maneuvers used by Allied surface combatants.
76. OA/NHC: *ComSubPac Patrol Report No. 627, U.S.S. Scabbardfish*-Second War Patrol, 3 January 1945.
77. Roscoe, *United States Submarine Operations in World War II*, p. 550.
78. *U.S. Submarine Losses-World War II*, p. 214.
79. OA/NHC: *ComSubPac Patrol Report No. 897, U.S.S. Spikefish*-Fourth War Patrol, 20 September 1945.
80. *U.S. Submarine Losses-World War II*, p. 177.

BIBLIOGRAPHY

Books

Barnett, Correlli. *Engage The Enemy More Closely*. W.W. Norton & Company, New York, 1991.

Churchill, Winston S. *Memoirs of the Second World War*. Houghton Mifflin Company, Boston, 1959.

Dönitz, Karl. *Memoirs: Ten Years and Twenty Days*. Naval Institute Press, Annapolis, 1990.

Evans, A.S., *Beneath the Waves*. William Kimber, London, 1986.

Gallery, Rear Admiral Daniel V., USN. *Twenty Million Tons Under the Sea*. Henry Regnery Company, Chicago, 1956.

Gibson, Charles. *The Ship With Five Names*. Abelard-Schuman, London, 1965.

Gleichauf, Justin F. *Unsung Heroes, The Naval Armed Guard in World War II*. Naval Institute Press, Annapolis, 1990.

Hashimoto, Mochitsura. *Sunk*. Cassell and Company Ltd., London, 1954.

Herlin, Hans. *Der Letzte Mann Von Der Doggerbank*. Wilhelm Heyne Verlag, Munchen, 1979.

Hughes, Terry and Costello, John. *The Battle of the Atlantic*. The Dial Press/James Wade, New York, 1977.

Jones, Geoffrey P. *U-Boat Aces And Their Fates*. William Kimber, London, 1988.

Krammer, Arnold. *Nazi Prisoners of War in America*. Stein and Day, New York, 1979.

Langmaid, Rowland. *The Med: The Royal Navy in the Mediterranean 1939-45*. The Batchworth Press, London, 1948.

Lew, Margie. "Faith, Hope-And Survival," *Gum Saan Journal*. Chinese Historical Society of Southern California, Los Angeles, 1978.

Lydecker, Ryck. *Pigboat*. Sweetwater Press, Duluth, MN, 1973.

Mason, John T., Jr. *The Atlantic War Remembered*. Naval Institute Press, Annapolis, 1990.

Masters, David. *In Peril on the Sea: War Exploits of Allied Seamen*. The Cresset Press, London, 1960.

Matthews, Peter. *The Guinness Book of Records 1993*. Facts on File, New York, 1993.

McCunn, Ruthanne Lum. *Sole Survivor*. Design Enterprises of San Francisco, San Francisco, 1985.

Moore, Captain Arthur R. *A Careless Word...A Needless Sinking*. American Merchant Marine Museum, Kings Point, New York, 1985.

Moore, John Hammond. *The Faustball Tunnel*. Random House, New York, 1978.

Morison, Samuel Eliot. *History of the United States Naval Operations in World War II, The Battle of the Atlantic September 1939-May 1943, Vol. 1*. Little Brown and Company, Boston, 1964.

Morison, Samuel Eliot. *The Atlantic Battle Won, May 1943-May 1945, Vol. X*. Little Brown and Company, Boston, 1956.

Mulligan, Timothy, Ed. *Records Relating to U-Boat Warfare, 1939-1945: Guides to the Microfilmed Records of the German Navy, 1850-1945: No. 2*. National Archives and Records Administration, Washington, D.C., 1985.

Naval History Division, Office of the Chief of Naval Operations, *United States Submarine Losses World War II*. Washington, 1963.

Potter, E.B. *Sea Power*. Naval Institute Press, Annapolis, 1981.

Ratigan, William. *Great Lakes Shipwrecks and Survivals*. William B. Eerdmans Publishing Company, 1983.

Rogers, Stanley. *Sailors at War*. George G. Harrap & Co. Ltd., London, 1942.

Rohwer, Jurgen. *Axis Submarine Successes 1939-1945*. Introductory material, trans. John A. Broadwin. Naval Institute Press, Annapolis, Maryland, 1983.

Roscoe, Theodore. *United States Destroyer Operations in World War II*. Naval Institute Press, Annapolis, Maryland, 1988.

Roscoe, Theodore. *United States Submarine Operations in World War II*. Naval Institute Press, Annapolis, Maryland, 1988.

Roskill, DSC, RN, Captain Stephen W. *The War at Sea, 1939-1945, 3 Vols*. Her Majesty's Stationery Office, London, 1954, 1956.

Rössler, Eberhard. *The U-Boat: The Evolution and Technical History of German Submarines*. Arms and Armor Press, London, 1981.

Ships of the Esso Fleet in World War II. Standard Oil Company of New Jersey, New York, 1946.

Showell, Jak P. Mallmann. *The German Navy in World War Two*, Naval Institute Press, Annapolis, 1979.

Showell, Jak P. Mallmann. *U-Boats Under the Swastika*. Naval Institute Press, Annapolis, 1987.

Smith, Peter C. and Walker, Edwin. *Sea Battles Close-up: The Battles of the Malta Striking Forces*. Naval Institute Press, Annapolis, 1974.

The Story of the U-505. Museum of Science and Industry, Chicago, 1981.

Vat, Dan van der. *The Atlantic Campaign: World War II's Great Struggle at Sea*. Harper & Row, New York, 1988.

Wheal, Elizabeth-Anne/Pope, Stephen/Taylor, James. *Encyclopedia of the Second World War*. Castle Books, New York, 1989.

Woodward, David. *The Secret Raiders*. W.V. Norton, New York, 1955.

Foreign and U.S. Government Documents

''Action Reports by U.S. Antisubmarine Patrol and Carrier Based Composite Squadrons,'' Operational Archives, Naval Historical Center, Washington, D.C.

ADM 199, Volumes 2130-2148, British Shipping Casualties Section/Trade Division: ''Reports of Interviews with Survivors of Shipping Casualties.''

''ComSubPac Patrol Report No. 627, *U.S.S. Scabbardfish*-Second War Patrol, 3 January 1945.'' Operational Archives, Naval Historical Center, Washington, D.C.

''ComSubPac Patrol Report No. 897, *U.S.S. Spikefish*-Fourth War Patrol, 20 September 1945.'' Operational Archives, Naval Historical Center, Washington, D.C.

''Ein Mann Uberlebt die Katastrophe von *U-183*'' (One Man Survives the Catastrophy of U 183). U-Boot Archive, Cuxhaven, Germany.

''Interrogation of Prisoner Taken from German Submarine U-183 Sunk by *U.S.S. Besugo* on 23 April 1945,'' Commanding Officer, Seventh Fleet Intelligence Center, May 31, 1945. Operational Archives, Naval Historical Center, Washington, D.C.

Kreigstagebücher (KTB) War Diary of *U-103*, 6, 7, 13 December 1942. National Archives Microfilm Publication T-1022, PG 30099/1-12, Rolls 3036-3037.

Kreigstagebücher (KTB) War Diary of *U-106*, 23 October 1941. National Archives Microfilm Publication T-1022, PG 30102/1-2, Roll 3034.

Kreigstagebücher (KTB) War Diary of *U-172*, 23 November 1942. National Archives Microfilm Publication T-1022, PG 30159/1-7, Roll 2885.

Kreigstagebücher (KTB) War Diary of *U-515*, 6, 7 December 1942. National Archives Microfilm Publication T-1022, PG 30553/1-6, Roll 3067.

HMS Medway 11, Recommendation for Decoration or Mention in Dispatches in the Case of John H. Capes, 14th July 1943.

Lloyd's War Losses: The Second World War, Vol. 1., British, Allied and Neutral Merchant Vessels Sunk or Destroyed by War Causes. Lloyd's of London Press Ltd., London, 1989.

''Naval Intelligence Division Reports of Interrogation of Axis Submarine and Merchant Ship Survivors,'' CNO/OPNAV Intelligence Series, World War II. Operational Archives, Naval Historical Center, Washington, D.C.

Oberkommando der Kriegsmarine (High Command German Navy), No. 1.SKL. Ik 13792/43 gKdos, RE: Loss of *Doggerbank*. Berlin, 15 May 1943.

''Prisoner of War Statements, Commander Submarine Force, Pacific Fleet,'' Command File World War II, Operational Archives, Naval Historical Center, Washington, D.C.

''Summaries of Statements of Survivors,'' National Archives and Records Administration, Washington, D.C. filed by ship. (RG 38).

''*U.S.S. Besugo (SS321)*, Report of Fourth Patrol, 20 May 1945,'' Operational Archives, Naval Historical Center, Washington, D.C.

U.S.S. Morrison (DD560), Action Report; Anti-Submarine Action by U.S.S. MORRISON (DD560), 31 March 1945, Operational Archives, Naval Historical Center, Washington, D.C.

Periodicals

Giese, Otto and Wise, James E., Jr. ''Hitler's U-Boats in The Pacific,'' *Sea Classics*, June 1991.

Gower, Rex. ''Ferry Survivor Re-lives Horror,'' *Evening Telegraph*, April 12, 1991.

Harby, Lt. Comdr. Samuel F., USNR. ''They Survived the Sea,'' *National Geographic Magazine*, May 1945.

London Gazette-1941: Commendation for L.A.L. Smith.

Pedrick, Clare. ''Italian Ferry, Oil Tanker Collide; 138 Feared Dead,'' *Washington Post*, April 12, 1991.

Saville, Allison W. ''German Submarines in The Far East.'' U.S. Naval Institute *Proceedings*, Annapolis, August 1961.

Williams, Dan and Schneider, Charles. ''Yarns of the Inland Seas,'' *The Cleveland Press*, April 29, 1945.

The Naval Institute Press is the book-publishing arm of the U.S. Naval Institute, a private, nonprofit, membership society for sea service professionals and others who share an interest in naval and maritime affairs. Established in 1873 at the U.S. Naval Academy in Annapolis, Maryland, where its offices remain today, the Naval Institute has members worldwide.

Members of the Naval Institute support the education programs of the society and receive the influential monthly magazine *Proceedings* or the colorful bimonthly magazine *Naval History* and discounts on fine nautical prints and on ship and aircraft photos. They also have access to the transcripts of the Institute's Oral History Program and get discounted admission to any of the Institute-sponsored seminars offered around the country.

The Naval Institute's book-publishing program, begun in 1898 with basic guides to naval practices, has broadened its scope to include books of more general interest. Now the Naval Institute Press publishes about seventy titles each year, ranging from how-to books on boating and navigation to battle histories, biographies, ship and aircraft guides, and novels. Institute members receive significant discounts on the Press's more than eight hundred books in print.

Full-time students are eligible for special half-price membership rates. Life memberships are also available.

For a free catalog describing Naval Institute Press books currently available, and for further information about joining the U.S. Naval Institute, please write to:

Member Services
U.S. Naval Institute
291 Wood Road
Annapolis, MD 21402-5034
Telephone: (800) 233-8764
Fax: (410) 571-1703
Web address: www.usni.org